MILLER'S HYMNAL

121 Favorite Hymns in
English and Ekpeye

By

Caroline Solomon Egbelu
Miller Tobia Solomon

Miller's Hymnal
121 Favorite Hymns in English and Ekpeye

Egbelu, Caroline Solomon
Solomon, Miller Tobia

Softcover: ISBN: 978-1-62971-002-0
E-Book: 978-1-62971-003-7
Published in the United States of America.

Library of Congress Control Number: 2023903897

Requests for permission should be sent to:
Jersey Publishing
info@jerseypublishing.com
Published by Jersey Publishing
www.jerseypublishing.com

Acknowledgement: Most of the hymns in this book were written before 1928 and are in public domain in the Unites States. As songs in public domain, we are allowed to scan, copy, distribute, arrange, adapt, or perform printed music from before 1928 without worrying about whether it is copyrighted. However, for those hymns that are not in public domain, permission has been obtained or in pending.

Dedication

This book is dedicated to my siblings who took care of our father in his old age. Thank you, Mrs. Esther Hezekiah (nee Orlunwo Miller), Dr. Ebube Solomon, Evangelist Blessing Ajayi (nee Uwuma Miller), Mr. Victor Solomon, Mrs. Sonia Shehu (nee Ununuma Solomon), Gbeji Solomon and Martha Solomon. Because of your display of love to our father, he lived happier and longer. May it be well with you and your families forever in Jesus Name.

--Caroline Solomon Egbelu

Appreciation

Many people helped to make the Miller's Hymnal possible. From those who typed and edited the manuscript to those who provided moral and financial support, we are grateful! Thank you, Professor Pius Egbelu, for all you did to make this book and other Solomon's publications a reality. We are indeed very grateful!

INTRODUCTION

Miller's Hymnal is a collection of hymns in English with translation to Ekpeye language. Each original English hymn was translated to Ekpeye and arranged to make it easier for the reader to read the lyrics in either English or Ekpeye language.

The translation from English to Ekpeye was done primarily to capture the meaning of the hymn lyrics for the Ekpeye speaker. This style of translation requires the reader to pay attention to hyphens used to separate words which are intended to produce the original tune of each hymn.

Ekpeye is a dialect spoken by people of Ekpeye Ethnic Nationality in Rivers State in the Niger Delta Region of Nigeria. Most Ekpeye communities are located between the Orashi and Sombriero rivers in Ahoada West and Ahoada East Local Government Areas.

Ekpeye shares boundary with Abua in the south, Ikwerre in the east, Ogba/Egbema in the north, and Engenni in the west. Politically, Ogba people are part of the Ogba/Egbema/Ndoni Local Government Area, which is in the northeast of Ekpeye and Abua people in Abua/Odual Local Government Area are in the south. Engenni people are part of Ahoada West Local Government Area. Ekpeye communities located along the Orashi River like Ombor, Oshiobele, and Akalamini, share boundary with the Engennis. Similarly, communities like Olokuma, Ikodu-Ekpeye and Odiereke-Ubie, located in the northwest of Ekpeye in Ubie Clan, share boundary and interact with Biseni people who are now part of the State of Bayelsa. The boundary between Rivers State and Bayelsa State from the west is in Engenni.

When we refer to the word "Ekpeye" in modern time, we mean diverse ways of identifying Ekpeye people and Ekpeye land.

Specifically, Ekpeye refers to a people, a language, a culture, and an ethnic group that reside within Ahoada East Local Government Area and Ahoada West Local Government Area of Rivers State in Nigeria in the continent of Africa.

Ekpeye as a language is still not in common use as a written language. It is not taught in schools and finding written communication in Ekpeye is still rare. Because Ekpeye language has not developed to compete with English even among fluent Ekpeye speakers, many struggle to pronounce written Ekpeye words. This is why it matters who did the translation of favorite hymns from English to Ekpeye language.

The translator, Miller Tobia Solomon, was an abstute and educated Ekpeye man who grew up in an Ekpeye family that valued and worked to preserved Ekpeye traditions and culture. An eloquent English and Ekpeye speaker, Solomon was the first person in Ubie Clan to complete a secondary school education when he graduated from the Azikiwe Institute of Commerce in Onitsha in 1955.

He was a continuous learner who craved knowledge. In 1978, he was admitted to study at the Hull College of Higher Education, a college of the University of Hull in England. Unfortunately, due to financial constraints, he was unable to fulfil that dream. Rather, he became a certified Professional Accountant as well as a Certified Professional Secretary through correspondence studies from the London School of Accountancy and the Rapid Result College in London. Solomon worked for several companies after graduation before settling as a farmer and businessman.
Solomon devoted his retirement years, between 2000 to 2010, to complete several manuscripts including The Chronicles of Ekpeye and Miller's Hymnal.

I am Miller Solomon's first daughter and a custodian of Miller Solomon's writings. It is my responsibility to coordinate my father's writings so the world would benefit from his knowledge.

As a coauthor, I usually work with a team of professionals to help me make my father's manuscripts, readable and applicable for Ekpeye readers as well as researchers of Ekpeye traditions and culture.

We welcome your questions, suggestions, and recommendations on ways to improve our work and encourage research in every aspect of Ekpeye studies.

--Caroline Solomon Egbelu

Figure 1: Map of Africa showing Nigeria
Source: Index Mundi online

Figure 2: Map of Nigeria showing Rivers State

Figure 3: Map of Rivers State showing 23 Local Government Areas including Ahoada East and Ahoada West Local Government Areas

Figure 4: Map of World showing Africa
Source: Freeworldmap.net

Figure 5: Map of Ekpeye

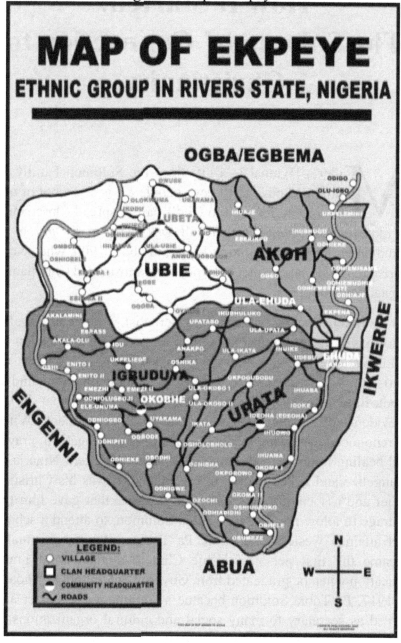

How It Started:
The Solomons' Connection to Christianity

Miller's Hymnal is a gift from the Solomon Family of Ikodu-Ekpeye to Ekpeye people. It is a symbol of our attempt to respond to God's call to spread Christianity in Ekpeye and beyond. That call was received by my great grandfather, Prophet Solomon Ekekpa, in about 1900, when early Christian missionaries entered Ekpeye and introduced Christianity to pagan worshippers.

Pa Solomon Ekekpa was a feared herbalist, a chief priest of a notorious shrine at Ikodu-Ekpeye and a very influential leader. Pa Solomon Ekekpa was one of the early Ekpeye converts to Christianity. The location of the ancestral Solomon compound at Ikodu-Ekpeye today, near the Orashi river and besides that shrine, is evidence of his allegiance to his paganistic assignment. When he renounced paganism, he devoted his life to evangelism, prayer and healing ministries. He travelled widely in eastern Nigeria to evangelize and called people to repentance. It was his Christian belief and association with early missionaries that gave him the courage to allow his first son, Tobia Solomon, to attend a school and attain a western education. Pa Tobia Solomon eventually became the first person in Ubie Clan to attain a sixth-grade education when he graduated from Government School at Ahoada in 1917. Pa Tobia Solomon became a community organizer and served as secretary to many social and cultural organizations in Ekpeye and around the neighboring ethnic groups. He was instrumental in coordinating the organized structure of Ekpeye traditions and culture as we know it in current times. Pa Tobia Solomon in turn educated his first son, Miller Tobia Solomon, who became the first Ubie person to complete a secondary school education.

The Solomons, like the children of biblical Israel, did not always following the calling of God in their lives but God never forgot them. Although they faced many trials and challenges in their lives, Pa Tobia Solomon and my father, Miller Solomon, never forgot their ambition to use their education for the betterment of Ekpeye people.

Pa Tobia Solomon began gathering material in 1921 to create a book of Ekpeye history so that younger generations would be familiai with the unique history and culture of Ekpeye. After his death on January 10, 1993, Miller Solomon continued the quest to produce a book of history. He completed a manuscript in 2004 that was the foundation of the book of Ekpeye history titled The Chronicles of Ekpeye. This book, Miller's Hymnal, is Miller Solomon's effort in help Ekpeye language speakers to read and sing their favorite hymns in their own language.

Our goal is that more written works, religious and traditional, would be translated to Ekpeye language to help Ekpeye speakers improve their knowledge of spoken and written Ekpeye language.

As a family, we can proclaim victory that the God who has seen us through the years will restore to us and release all the blessings withheld. We claim Psalm 121, as we glorify our God, the heavenly father, who called our patriarch, Solomon Ekpekpa, out of paganism into freedom in Christ Jesus!

Psalm 121 NIV (Modified)

"We will lift up our eyes to the hills—
From whence comes our help?
2 Our help comes from the LORD,
Who made heaven and earth.

3 He will not allow our feet to [a]be moved;
He who keeps us will not slumber.
4 Behold, He who keeps Israel
Shall neither slumber nor sleep.

5 The LORD is our [b]keeper;
The LORD is our shade at our right hand.
6 The sun shall not strike us by day,
Nor the moon by night.

7 The LORD shall [c]preserve us from all evil;
He shall preserve our soul.
8 The LORD shall preserve[d] our going out and our coming in
From this time forth, and even forevermore."

--Caroline Solomon Egbelu

INDEX OF HYMNS

Miller Hymnal (MH) Number	SDA Hymn Number	HYMN TITLE	MH Page Number.
1	73	Holy, Holy, Holy	18
2	197	The King of Love My Shepherd Is	20
3	218	When He Cometh	22
4	567	Have thine Own Way	24
5	522	My Hope is Built on Nothing Less	26
6	86	How Great Thou Art	28
7	281	I Gave my Life for Thee	30
8	462	Blessed Assurance	32
9	625	Higher Ground	34
10	618	Stand Up, Stand Up	36
11	108	Amazing Grace	38
12	51	Day is Dying in the West	40
13	422	Marching to Zion	42
14	103	O God, Our Help	44
15	485	I Must Tell Jesus	46
16	341	To God Be the Glory	48
17	39	Lord, In the Morning	50
18	359	Hark, the Voice of Jesus	52
19	295	Chief of Sinners	56
20	213	Jesus is Coming	58
21	458	More Love to Thee	60
22	245	More About Jesus	62
23	331	O Jesus, I Have Promised	64
24	296	Lord, I'm Coming Home	66
25	238	How Sweet the Name	70
26	549	Loving Shepherd of Thy Sheep	72
27	243	King Of Glory, King Of Peace	74
28	375	Work for the Night	76

Miller Hymnal (MH) Number	SDA Hymn Number	HYMN TITLE	MH Page Number.
29	369	Bringing in the Sheaves	78
30	52	Now the Day is Over	80
31	463	Peace Perfect Peace	82
32	50	Abide with Me	84
33	4	Praise, My Soul, thy King of Heaven	86
34	21	Immortal, Invisible, God Only Wise	88
35	83	O Worship the King	90
36	93	All Things Bright and Beautiful	92
37	99	God will Take Care of You	94
38	107	God Moves in a Mysterious Way	96
39	154	When I Survey the Wondrous Cross	98
40	160	Ride on in Majesty	100
41	82	Before Jehovah's Awful Throne	102
42	190	Jesus Loves Me	104
43	221	Rejoice, The Lord is King	106
44	227	Jesus Shall Reign	108
45	229	All Hail the Power of Jesus	110
46	230	All Glory Loud and Honor	112
47	241	Jesus, The Very Thought of Thee	114
48	254	The Great Physician	116
49	267	Spirit Divine	118
50	279	Only Trust Him	120
51	286	Wonderful Words of Life	122
52	287	Softly and Tenderly	124
53	300	Rock of Ages	126
54	304	Faith of our Fathers	128
55	306	Draw me Nearer	130

Miller Hymnal (MH) Number	SDA Hymn Number	HYMN TITLE	MH Page Number
56	309	All to Jesus I Surrender	132
57	294	Power in the Blood	134
58	312	Near the Cross	136
59	313	Just As I Am	138
60	321	My Jesus, I Love Thee	140
61	330	Take My Life and Let It Be	142
62	340	Jesus Saves	144
63	343	I Will Sing of My Redeemer	148
64	272	Give Me the Bible	150
65	465	I Heard the Voice of Jesus	152
66	327	I'd Rather Have Jesus	154
67	517	My Faith Looks Up to Thee	156
68	420	Jerusalem, My Happy Home	158
69	428	Sweet By and By	160
70	445	I'm But a Stranger Here	162
71	469	Leaning on the Everlasting Arms	164
72	470	There's Sunshine in My Soul Today	166
73	473	Nearer my God, To Thee	168
74	478	Sweet Hour of Prayer	170
75	483	I Need Thee Every Hour	172
76	489	Jesus, Lover of My Soul	174
77	499	What a Friend We have in Jesus	178
78	502	Sun of My Soul	180
79	518	Standing on the Promises	182
80	530	It is Well With My Soul	184
81	64	Lord Dismiss Us With Thy Blessing	186
82	537	He Leadeth Me	188
83	538	Guide, Me O Thou Great Jehovah	190

Miller Hymnal (MH) Number	SDA Hymn Number	HYMN TITLE	MH Page Number
84	561	We Plow the Fields	192
85	569	Pass Me Not, O Gentle Savior	194
86	590	Trust and Obey	196
87	603	Christian, Seek Not Repose	198
88	638	The Wise May Bring Their Learning	200
89	612	Onward, Christian Soldiers	202
90	71	Come Thou Almighty King	204
91	112	Let Us with A Gladsome Mind	206
92	132	O Come, All Ye Faithful	208
93	143	Silent Night, Holy Night	210
94	166	Christ the Lord is Risen	212
95	672	Spirit of the Living God	214
96	694	Praise God from Whom All Blessings	216
97	121	Go, Tell It On The Mountain	218
98	139	While Shepherd Watched Their Flocks	220
99	216	When the Roll is Called Up Yonder	222
100	318	Whiter Than Snow	224
101	172	The Strife is Over	226
102	195	Showers of Blessings	228
103	165	Look, Ye Saints the Sight in Glorious	230
104	461	Be Still My Soul	234
105	65	God Be With You	236
106	248	O How I Love Jesus	238
107	374	Jesus, with Thy Church Abide	240
108	432	Shall We Gather at the River	242
109	159	Thy Old Rugged Cross	244

Miller Hymnal (MH) Number	SDA Hymn Number	HYMN TITLE	MH Page Number
110	557	Come, Ye Thankful People	246
111	336	There is a Fountain	250
112	526	Because He Lives	254
113	246	Worthy, Worthy is The Lamb	256
114	600	Hold Fast Till I Come	258
115	623	I Will Follow Thee	260
116	100	Great Is Thy Faithfulness	262
117	164	There is a Green Far Away	264
118	559	Now Thank We Our God	266
119	653	Lead Them, My God, To Thee	268
120	692	The Lord is in His Holy Temple	270
121	660	Glory Be To The Father	272

MH 1   Holy, Holy, Holy   SDAH 73

Reginald Heber, 1826, (1783-1826)
English

1
Holy, Holy, Holy! Lord God Almighty!
Early in the morning our song shall rise to Thee;
Holy, holy, holy, merciful and mighty!
God in three persons, blessed Trinity!

2
Holy, Holy, Holy! Angels adore Thee,
Casting down their bright crowns around the glassy sea;
Thousands and ten thousands worship low before Thee,
Which wert, and art, and evermore shalt be.

3
Holy, Holy, Holy! though the darkness hide Thee,
Though the eye of man Thy great glory may not see;
Only Thou art holy; there is none beside Thee,
Perfect in power, in love, and purity.

4
Holy, Holy, Holy! Lord God Almighty!
All Thy works shall praise Thy name, in earth, and sky, and sea;
Holy, holy, holy; merciful and mighty!
God in three persons, blessed Trinity!

MH 1   Holy, Holy, Holy   SDAH 73
Reginald Heber, 1826, (1783-1826)
Ekpeye Translation

1
Egwele, egwele, egwele! Eblikpabi kakpoligbe
Lime Oyukwe orbuye eja eka yo;
Egwele, egwele, egwele, nye ortu izhi linye eke obu-eke!
Ebilikpabi zheli madu itor, uzugbani zhi uwakwani!

2
Egwele, egwele, egwele! Emene zhi egwele kpeni gbe yo,
Kpumagbe okpulu ishi eze gbe lwukwu olimini onyo,
U-nu kwulu u-nu jini gbeyo ukpu nu uko,
Amu uzhor muzhi dhi dhor, Le-ke o-gbo ogbo.

3
Egwele, egwele, egwele! Igeleni woke yo,
Enye madu egedhe notor igili gbaka ma-ayo,
Yo neten zhi egwele; udiye zhe dhe gba,
I-zuke lu ugbakpo, ugwushi lu uzhi eso.

4.
Egwele, egwele, egwele! Eblikpabi kakpoligbe
Eka Ugboloyo padhiye ewa yo luwa, lolu, lolimini
Egwele, egwele, egwele! Note ortu izhi linye eke obeke
Eblikpabi zheli madu itor, uzugbani zhi uwokwani

MH 2   The King of Love My Shepherd   SDAH 197

H. W. Baker, 1868 (1821-1877)

English

1

The King of love my Shepherd is,
His goodness faileth never;
I nothing lack if I am His,
And He is mine forever.

2

Where streams of living water flow
My ransomed soul He leadeth,
And, where the verdant pastures grow,
With food celestial feedeth.

3

Perverse and foolish, oft I strayed,
But yet in love He sought me,
And on His shoulder gently laid,
And home, rejoicing, brought me.

4

And so through all the length of days
Thy goodness faileth never;
Good Shepherd! I would sing Thy praise
Within Thy house forever.

MH 2   The King of Love My Shepherd   SDAH 197
H. W. Baker, 1868 (1821-1877)
Ekpeye Translation

1
Eze ugwushi nyudu me bu,
Iye uma ya gbono o-gbo,
Iye Iye korshe me lam bule aya,
Ubu aame leke ogbo ogbo.

2
Adhi mini mu budu ugbor
Ekpema mugor yabu nyo odua,
Ika mu ushi uma zorlorgbe,
Ghidhi orbioma bu iye edhi gbe.

3
Morbu nyuukpega li nyi-shi,
Lime ugwushi mu uwudhi ga me,
Leweka ya mubu dhi me,
Le ekpema etor mu lawe me udhor

4
Lime gbe-le gbele e-ye,
Iye-uma ya gbono ogbo
Nyu udume! morgwu nyi orbu upadhi,
Lu udhor ya gbe-le gbele ekele

MH 3   When He Cometh   SDAH 218

W. O. Chushing, 1866(1873-1903)

English

1
When He cometh, when He cometh
To make up His jewels,
All His jewels, precious jewels,
His loved and His own.

Chorus

Like the stars of the morning,
His brightness adorning,
They shall shine in their beauty,
Bright gems for His crown.

2
He will gather, He will gather
The gems for His kingdom;
All the pure ones, all the bright ones,
His loved and His own.

3
Little children, little children,
Who love their Redeemer,
Are the jewels, precious jewels,
His loved and His own.

MH 3   When He Cometh   SDAH 218
W. O. Chushing, 1866(1873-1903)
Ekpeye Translation

1
Eke ejor, eke ejor
Lukpo gbedhe igwu ezorya,
Ogbo igwu ezor, Ekpuligwu gbu aya
Amu ugwushor mu unyo

Chorus
Kpumu Okpudhor egbuluka Oyukwe,
Akpu okplishi eze ya sale,
Akpu sale lezor gbe,
Okplishi ekpligwu ezor.

2
Okpe gbedhe, okpo gbedhe
Ekpligwu ezor le ele eze ya;
Otu uma mu, otu eke usam,
Amu ugwushor mu unyo.

3
Umeledhe, Umeledhe,
Mu ugwushe gbe nye gbe,
Ubugbe igwu ezor ekpligwu gbu aya,
Amu ugwushor mu unyo.

MH 4　　Have Thine Own Way　　SDAH 567

Adelaide Pollard (1862-1934)

English

1

Have thine own way, Lord! Have thine own way!
Thou art the potter, I am the clay.
Mold me and make me after thy will,
while I am waiting, yielded and still.

2

Have thine own way, Lord! Have thine own way!
Search me and try me, Savior today!
Wash me just now, Lord, wash me just now,
as in thy presence humbly I bow.

3

Have thine own way, Lord! Have thine own way!
Wounded and weary, help me I pray!
Power, all power, surely is thine!
Touch me and heal me, Savior divine!

4

Have thine own way, Lord! Have thine own way!
Hold o'er my being absolute sway.
Fill with thy Spirit till all shall see
Christ only, always, living in me!

MH 4   Have Thine Own Way   SDAH 567
Adelaide Pollard (1862-1934)
Ekpeye Translation

1
Me echi che yo, Eda! Me echiche yo!
Ibu nyor kpu ite, morbu uza ya,
Kpu mu mime mu, kpu umashi yo,
Kpom medhu sejor, lu uwhedanyi
.

2
Me echiche yo, Eda! me echiche yo!
Domu mi maa mu, edanwu-dhor me tam!
Ka mini orkpor eligwe, samam lu umorm,
Kpu zhile lu ununu yo, lu sorbia nyi.

3
Me echiche yo, Eda! Me echiche yo!
Umedhu meli li ike ugwulu, gworm, mor dhor yo,
Ugbakpo li gbele gbele ugbakpo, ubu ayo!
Kportum mi gormu, nyu gawe zhi eso!

4
Me echiche yo, Eda! Me echiche yo!
Mojike bu-du me, Li gbele gbele uhkwu,
Shishi mu uwa yo me enye ogbo notu,
Christ neten gbele gbele ekele, zhili ime me!

MH 5   My Hope is Built on Nothing Less   SDAH 522
Edward Mote 1834(1797-1874)
English

1
My hope is built on nothing less
than Jesus' blood and righteousness.
I dare not trust the sweetest frame,
but wholly lean on Jesus' name.

Chorus
On Christ the solid rock I stand;
all other ground is sinking sand,
all other ground is sinking sand.

2
When Darkness seems to veil His face,
I rest on his unchanging grace.
in every high and stormy gale,
my anchor holds within the veil.
3
His oath, his covenant, his blood
supports me in the whelming flood.
When all around my soul gives way,
he then is all my hope and stay.
4
When He shall come with trumpet sound,
O may I then in him be found!
Dressed in his righteousness alone,
faultless to stand before the throne.

MH 5 My Hope is Built on Nothing Less SDAH 522
Edward Mote 1834(1797-1874)
Ekpeye Translation

1
Unye enye me zheli iye iye
Gama ubala umam Jesus.
Ndeke mortu kwashiem iye,
Etar obu, Ma dabeni lewa Jesus.

Chorus
Christ bu olu-igwu monuzo;
Udor ele dhi ligbe edhili,
Udor ele dhi ligbe edhili.

2
Eke Igeleni u-da-le,
Mezhi lortu izhiya enye- ugbanyo.
Le, gbele gbele eke uwele,
Umoji eka me zhi li ya.

3
Orwo li egba li ubala ya
Dorkpewe me leke miniji.
Kporm gbele gbele iye lorkpo gbeme,
Yo neten bu nye zhinyi me.

4
Eke ejor luli okpor ordu,
Uwu eji gbeme leli ya,
Lu uzhe neten liyuma ya,
Le ortu ikpe unuzo lagida Eze ya.

MH 6   How Great Thou Art   SDAH 86

Stuart K Hine (1899-)

English

1

O Lord my God, When I in awesome wonder
Consider all the worlds Thy Hands have made
I see the stars I hear the rolling thunder
Thy power throughout the universe displayed.

Chorus

Then sings my soul, My Saviour God to Thee
How great Thou art, How great Thou art
Then sings my soul, My Saviour God to Thee
How great Thou art, How great Thou art

2

When through the woods, And Forest glades I wander
And hear the birds sing sweetly in the trees
When I look down. From lofty mountain grandeur
And see the brook and feel the gentle breeze

3

And when I think That God His Son not sparing
Sent Him to die I scarce can take it in
That on the Cross My burden gladly bearing
He bled and died to take away my sin.

4

When Christ shall come With shouts of acclamation
And take me home What joy shall fill my heart
Then I shall bow In humble adoration
And there proclaim "My God, how great Thou art!"

MH 6   How Great Thou Art   SDAH 86

Stuart K Hine (1899-)

Ekpeye Translation

1
Eblikpabi, Ekeme nye le otu ogwu le eso
Lugbeji uwam eka yo mor,
Orkpudhor egbuluka le, Ekpor uhgbadhe amaa,
Ugbakpo yo gbe le eluwa logbo.

Chorus
Uwame gwuobum, nyu, Ugaweme nye nwe ye
Obueke yo, Obueke yo
Uwame gwuobum nyu, Ugaweme nye nwe ye
Obueke yo! Obueke yo!

2
Eke maga dhiga lime ukaya,
Mornuji orbu etor ogbo unu gwugbe lu ushi
Me nye da ele, Leke olu egbu,
Me weji mini le etor uwakayi uma.

3
Eke mechele, Kpu eda ugwele uwhe unwa
Uzha gbu nwulu enwu me whetor mu,
Lu ushi uye lu uka, Lubuji umekpeli me,
Unwulu enwu luma umeyeshi me.

4
Christ ejor leke ikpu
Upadhi, nde obu etor me
Leke alawe me udhor
Me kpenya leke usorbiya ni,
Maka Ebilikpabi O obueke Yo!

MH 7   I Gave my Life for Thee   SDAH 281

Francis Ridley Havergal, 1858 (1836-1879)

English

1

I gave my life for thee,
My precious blood I shed,
That thou might'st ransom be,
And quickened from the dead;
I gave, I gave My life for thee,
What hast thou given for Me?
I gave, I gave My life for thee,
What hast thou given for Me?

2

My Father's house of light,
My glory circled throne,
I left for earthly night,
For wanderings sad and lone;
I left, I left it all for thee,
Hast thou left aught for Me?
I left, I left it all for thee,
Hast thou left aught for Me?

3

I suffered much for thee,
more than thy tongue can tell,
Of bitterest agony,
To rescue thee from hell;
I've borne, I've borne it all for thee,
What hast thou borne for Me?
I've borne, I've borne it all for thee,
What hast thou borne for Me?

MH 7   I Gave my Life for Thee   SDAH 281
Francis Ridley Havergal, 1858 (1836-1879)
Ekpeye Translation

1
Me ne budu me liyo,
Ubalame womo sor,
Kpemele Mordor yo,
Meke ile lo enwu,
Mene budu liyo,
Nde ıye imenyi me?
Mene budu liyo,
Nde iye imenyi me?

2
Udhor usamali Eda me,
Agida eze igili me,
Morlor labali uwa,
Lu ugadhiga lagbezhi,
Gbele gbelem me gbeni yo
Ye gbeni leme kpe?
Gbele gbelem me gbeni yo
Ye gbeni leme kpe?

3
Maata nyi yo akwukwu,
Ka kpu idho yo aba le,
Li ilu le eke agbezhi,
Lu udor kpewe yo lechi,
Gbele gbelem mobunyi liyo,
Nde iye ibunyi me?
Gbele gbelem mobunyi liyo,
Nde iye ibunyi me?

MH 8   **Blessed Assurance**   SDAH 462

Fanny J. Crosby, 1873 (1820-1915)

English

1
Blessed assurance, Jesus is mine!
O what a foretaste of glory divine!
Heir of salvation, purchase of God,
born of his Spirit, washed in his blood.

Chorus
This is my story, this is my song,
praising my Savior all the day long;
this is my story, this is my song,
praising my Savior all the day long.

2
Perfect submission, perfect delight,
visions of rapture now burst on my sight;
angels descending bring from above
echoes of mercy, whispers of love.

3
Perfect submission, all is at rest;
I in my Savior am happy and blest,
watching and waiting, looking above,
filled with his goodness, lost in his love.

MH 8   Blessed Assurance   SDAH 462

Fanny J. Crosby, 1873 (1820-1915)

Ekpeye Translation

1
Egba Uwokwani, Jesus bu ame!
Amu edhi wejor li igili uwa esor!
Nwe nye ugawe, Eblikpabi gor,
Umagbe limi uwa esor, sama limi ubala

Chorus
Ombu udhor kala me, ombu orbu me,
Padhiwe nyu gawe me gbele gbele eye,
Ombu udhor kala me, ombu orbu me
Padhiwe nyu gawe me gbele gbele eye.

2
Egedhe usorbianyi, egedhe obu etor
Gbudhor unye iye obuetor lor lu ununu me,
Emene uzhi Eblikpabi uja gbe lolu
Ugalagbe Uwhotuzhi, lu takwu kala ugwushi

3
Egedhe usorbia niji, ezhi kpole gbe,
Me li ime nyu gawe me uwakwani li obu etor,
Use adhi lu useji, lu unye, enye lolu,
Yuluka liye uma ya, udhili li ugwushi

MH 9   Higher Ground   SDAH 625

Joseph Oatman, Jr. (1856-1922)

English

1

I'm pressing on the upward way,
New heights I'm gaining every day;
Still praying as I'm onward bound,
"Lord, plant my feet on higher ground."

Chorus
Lord, lift me up and let me stand,
By faith, on Heaven's table land,
A higher plane than I have found;
Lord, plant my feet on higher ground.

2

My heart has no desire to stay
Where doubts arise and fears dismay;
Though some may dwell where those abound,
My prayer, my aim, is higher ground.

3

I want to live above the world,
Though Satan's darts at me are hurled;
For faith has caught the joyful sound,
The song of saints on higher ground.

4

I want to scale the utmost height
And catch a gleam of glory bright;
But still I'll pray till Heav'n I've found,
"Lord, plant my feet on higher ground."

MH 9   Higher Ground   SDAH 625
Joseph Oatman, Jr. (1856-1922)
Ekpeye Translation

1
Me zhi lu ugbake lu uka ze olu
Gbele gbele eye, me zhi lu uka ze,
Me zhi ludhor, kporm makazor,
"Nye nwe ye gbete mu lu olu egbu."

Chorus
Gbabuzem olu, meke nnuzo,
Lime uwhetu, le ele orbioma
Li olu egbu, ka adhim mezhor,
Nye nwe ye gbete mu lo olu egbu

2
Ekpema me, wudhiga unazhi
La adhi orwele lo otogwu zhi,
Ubotu ebegbe la adhi zhikpe,
Edhor le anwa me zhi o-lu egbu

3
Mo wudhi ga ube ka etor uwa,
Ulu ekpesu, le elime kike,
Uwhetu ayawele, uli etor uma
Orbu emene uzhi uma zhi lo olu egbu

4
Mo wudhi ga, ukaze echi olu,
Lu weji igili usamali
Umom medhu dhor, lu uwu- eji orbioma,
Nye nwe ye duze- mu olu egbu

MH 10   Stand Up, Stand Up   SDAH 618

George Duffield, 1858 (1818-1888)

English

1

Stand up, stand up for Jesus! ye soldiers of the cross;
Lift high His royal banner, it must not suffer loss:
From vict'ry unto vict'ry, His army shall He lead,
Till every foe is vanquished, and Christ is Lord indeed.

2

Stand up, stand up for Jesus! The trumpet call obey:
Forth to the mighty conflict, in this His glorious day;
Ye that are men now serve Him against unnumbered foes;
Let courage rise with danger, and strength to strength oppose.

3

Stand up, stand up for Jesus! Stand in His strength alone,
The arm of flesh will fail you, ye dare not trust your own;
Put on the gospel armor, and watching unto prayer,
Where calls the voice of duty, be never wanting there.

4

Stand up, stand up for Jesus! the strife will not be long;
This day the noise of battle, the next the victor's song;
To him that overcometh a crown of life shall be;
He with the King of glory shall reign eternally.

MH 10   Stand Up, Stand Up   SDAH 618
George Duffield, 1858 (1818-1888)
Ekpeye Translation

1

Nuzo nuzo nyi nyi Jesus! emenulu ushi uye luka,
Gbabuzeni unazi eze ya, ndeke ada la awa:
Godhu lu umegbo dhuma udor umegbo,
Yewe odu emene a-wa ya,
Tutu emene egba gwulu kpogbe,
Christ bu egedhe nye nwe-ye.

2

Nuzo nuzo nyi nyi Jesus!Ze uwhu ordu ulu gbuhu
Le unazhi e-ke orwele mu, le eye upadhi ma Aya
Lu morm, emene a-ya lugboni ogbo emene egba,
Menyi mobu yo ke-i-ke, mu ugbakpo nye egba da

3

Nuzo nuzo nyi nyi Jesus, nuzo lu ugbako ya, ugbakpo
Madu anagbo yo, eborne ugbakpo yo,
Gonu iye ulu uzhi uma, sejike lime edhor,
Adhi ugbolo liye ike whule yo, Eme mu egwe uzedho.

4

Nuzo, nuzo nyi nyi Jesus! ulum ndeke odhu ubie,
Tam bu eye uwhu a-wa, ude eye bu orbu umegbo
Nye mu megbodhi emegbo okpulishi budu be aya;
Nye ya li Eze igili, uchigbe gwulu orgwulu.

MH 11   Amazing Grace   SDAH 108

John Newton, 1779 (1725-1807)

English

1

Amazing grace!
How sweet the sound
that saved a wretch like me!
I once was lost, but now am found;
was blind, but now I see.

2

'Twas grace that taught my heart to fear,
and grace my fears relieved;
how precious did that grace appear
the hour I first believed.

3

The Lord has promised good to me,
his word my hope secures;
he will my shield and portion be,
as long as life endures.

4

Through many dangers, toils, and snares,
I have already come;
'tis grace hath brought me safe thus far,
and grace will lead me home.

5

When we've been there ten thousand years,
bright shining as the sun,
we've no less days to sing God's praise
than when we first begun.

MH 11   Amazing Grace   SDAH 108
John Newton, 1779 (1725-1807)
Ekpeye Translation

1
Ortizhi unwo dhe enye!
Ndekpu etor ya zhile,
Amu gawor nyu uya kpumu me!
Mo wulu kpolem, lumorm mor lorlem,
Enye ukpolime, onotule adhi.

2
Otizhim zhi ekpema me kpu utule otogu,
Ortizhi mu ugwor otogu me,
Ndekpu ibala ortizhi zhile,
Ekemu me whetor.

3
Nye nwe ye gwu nye me egbuma,
Le ekpor ya uwhetu me zuke,
Orbunyi me okpulishi ulu
Kpu budu me zhile.

4
Lime ogbo otogu la akwukwu,
Ma galem li ime ya,
Otizhi ordorkpewe le me.
Ortizhi odu mu udhor.

5
Eke azhi ladhi ya unu ogbo ogbo,
Adhi samali kpormu eleanwu
Gbele gbele eye apadhi we eda ye,
Kakpu eye unuzu.

MH 12   Day is Dying in the West   SDAH 51
Mary A. Lathbury, 1877 (1841-1913)
English

1
Day is dying in the west;
Heaven is touching earth with rest;
Wait and worship while the night
Sets the evening lamps alight
Through all the sky.

Chorus
Holy, holy, holy, Lord God of Hosts!
Heaven and earth are full of Thee!
Heaven and earth are praising Thee,
O Lord most high!

2
Lord of life, beneath the dome
Of the universe, Thy home,
Gather us who seek Thy face
To the fold of Thy embrace,
For Thou art nigh.

3
While the deepening shadows fall,
Heart of love enfolding all,
Through the glory and the grace
Of the stars that veil Thy face,
Our hearts ascend.
4
When forever from our sight
Pass the stars, the day, the night,
Lord of angels, on our eyes
Let eternal morning rise
And shadows end.

MH 12   Day is Dying in the West   SDAH 51
Mary A. Lathbury, 1877 (1841-1913)
Ekpeye Translation

1
Eye udhu nwulu ligbu uda,
Orbioma udhu ne uwa udeli
Seji mu ikpeni leke abali
Mu-shile tonjor ya li ela,
Ligbe-le gbele olu.

Chorus
Egwele, egwele, egwele, Eblikpabi nyo ogbo
Orbioma luwa yulugbe liyo
Orbioma luwa padhiwe gbeyo,
Eblikpabi ka-kpo-ligbe!

2
Eblikpabi budu zhile eluwa
Imewe gbele gbele uwa, Imudhor yo,
Megbedhe ye emene mu awudhiga yo,
Le-eliyo hushi yo, Izhi lu uzedhu.

3
Leke madu dalegbe linyina
Ekpema ugwushi megbedhe legbe,
Le-upadhi le-ortizhi, okpudor egbuluka lorwe gbe upi gbe,
Ekpema ye la olu.

4
Lekele ubuzelile lienyeye
Okpudhor egbuluka, eye li abali,
Nyishi uzhi uma le ekpeleni ye,
Oyukwu ogbo ogbo nuzo,
Me ainye gwulu gbe.

MH 13   Marching to Zion   SDAH 422
Isaac Watts, 1707 (1674-1748)

English

1

Come, we that love the Lord,
And let our joys be known;
Join in a song with sweet accord,
Join in a song with sweet accord,
And thus surround the throne,
And thus surround the throne.

Chorus
We're marching to Zion, Beautiful, beautiful Zion;
We're marching upward to Zion, The beautiful city of God.

2

Let those refuse to sing
Who never knew our God;
But children of the heav'nly King,
But children of the heav'nly King
May speak their joys abroad,
May speak their joys abroad.

3

The hill of Zion yields
A thousand sacred sweets
Before we reach the heav'nly fields,
Before we reach the heav'nly fields
Or walk the golden streets,
Or walk the golden streets.

4

Then let our songs abound
And ev'ry tear be dry;
We're marching thru Immanuel's ground,
We're marching thru Immanuel's ground
To fairer worlds on high,
To fairer worlds on high.

MH 13   Marching to Zion   SDAH 422
Isaac Watts, 1707 (1674-1748)
Ekpeye Translation

1
Jani emene mu agwushor Nye nwe ye,
Mumajigbe Ekpema etor ye,
Jani lunu orbu etor,
Jani lunu orbu etor,
Mashikoshi agida eze
Mashikoshi agida eze.

Chorus
Ya aka ze le Zion
Ula ezor ula ezor Zion
Ya aka ze le olu ula Zion
Ula ezor mu Eblikpabi

2
Emene mu ewhegbe ugwu
Umajegbe Nye nwe ye,
Umeledhe Eze orbioma
Umeledhe Eze orbioma,
Aka lor shie gbe obu etorgbe
Aka lor shie gbe obu etorgbe
3
Egbu Zion, orlu-wele,
Ogbo iye uma torgbetor,
Ma abaa dhuma ele orbioma
Ma abaa dhuma ele orbioma
Ma ga dhiga lichakpa gold
Ma ga dhiga lichakpa gold;

MH 14   O God Our Help   SDAH 103

Isaac Watts, 1707 (1674-1748)

English

1

O God, our help in ages past,
our hope for years to come,
our shelter from the stormy blast,
and our eternal home!

2

Under the shadow of thy throne,
still may we dwell secure;
sufficient is thine arm alone,
and our defense is sure.

3

Before the hills in order stood,
or earth received her frame,
from everlasting, thou art God,
to endless years the same.

4

A thousand ages, in thy sight,
are like an evening gone;
short as the watch that ends the night,
before the rising sun.

5

O God, our help in ages past,
our hope for years to come;
be thou our guide while life shall last,
and our eternal home!

MH 14   O God Our Help   SDAH 103
Isaac Watts, 1707 (1674-1748)
Ekpeye Translation

1
Eda ushie eka ye lukani
Unye enye ye lu ununu
Nye nyeke ye leke uwele
Udhor yem ogwulu gwulu

2
Lukpudhu agida eze
Mayo ya beshi likashi,
Uzuke zhi leka ma yo
Nye udoh budu ye.

3
Lununu egbum inuzotor,
Uwa natu unazhi,
Ibu Eblikpabi orgwulu
Orgwulu dhuma eke Ogbo ogbo

4
Ogbo unu ala lununu Yo
Zhikorm ela gaga
Ntuko kporm eye glu we abali
Ma elanwu mu ba wa

5
Eda ushie eka ye lukani
Unye enye ye lununu
Nyeke ye kpu budu ye dhuma le,
Udhor yem orgwulu orgwulu

MH 15   I Must Tell Jesus   SDAH 485

Elisha A. Hoffman, (1839-1929)
English

1
I must tell Jesus all of my trials,
I cannot bear these burdens alone;
In my distress He kindly will help me,
He ever loves and cares for His own.

Chorus
I must tell Jesus! I must tell Jesus!
I cannot bear my burdens alone;
I must tell Jesus! I must tell Jesus!
Jesus can help me, Jesus alone.

2
I must tell Jesus all of my troubles,
He is a kind, compassionate Friend;
If I but ask Him He will deliver,
Make of my troubles quickly an end.

3
Oh, how the world to evil allures me!
Oh, how my heart is tempted to sin!
I must tell Jesus, and He will help me
Over the world the vict'ry to win.

MH 15   I Must Tell Jesus   SDAH 485
Elisha A. Hoffman, (1839-1929)
Ekpeye Translation

1
Mokuni Jesus gbele gbele umama,
mobuji dhomu ubum meneten,
Umekpeli me sikeji mu eka,
Ugwushi emene ya unyeshi gbe enye;

Chorus
Mokuni Jesus, Mokuni Jesus
Mobuji dhomu ubun meneten
Mokuni Jesus, Mokuni Jesus
Sikeji mu eka Jesus neten

2
Mokuni Jesus umekpeli me,
Ya-we bu nwuje, nye nwe ugwushi,
ubule mokunya, ordorkpewe me,
mu umekpeli me meke ugbogbo

3
Emene eluwa kpayagbe gbiyor,
Umemu ekpema me mu nwe umeyeshi,
Mokuni Jesus sikeji mu eka
Me megbo emegbo, lime eluwa

MH 16   To God Be the Glory   SDAH 341

Fanny J. Crosby, 1875 (1820-1915)

English

1
To God be the glory, great things he hath done!
So loved he the world that he gave us his Son,
who yielded his life an atonement for sin,
and opened the lifegate that all may go in.

Chorus
Praise the Lord, praise the Lord,
let the earth hear his voice!
Praise the Lord, praise the Lord,
let the people rejoice!
O come to the Father thru Jesus the Son,
and give him the glory, great things he hath done!

2
O perfect redemption, the purchase of blood,
to every believer the promise of God;
the vilest offender who truly believes,
that moment from Jesus a pardon receives.

3
Great things he hath taught us, great things he hath done,
and great our rejoicing thru Jesus the Son;
but purer, and higher, and greater will be
our wonder, our transport, when Jesus we see.

MH 16   To God Be the Glory   SDAH 341

Fanny J. Crosby, 1875 (1820-1915)

Ekpeye Translation

1

Padhiwe, Eblikpabi, Leke, Iye mumor,
Lugwushi Uwa mune ye u-nwo ya,
Nye mu ne budu Ya lusor eja Umeyeshi,
mugwuma akwu budu muwa kpudhugbe

Chorus
Padhiwe Eda padhiwe Eda
mu uwa muji uli ya,
Padhiwe Eda padhiwe Eda,
mu madu padhigbe,
Kaja keji Eda lewa unwa Jesus,
Nedha upadhi leke i-ye mu umor.

2

Egedhe udorkpewe, Gowegbe ubala,
li nye whetule legba Eblikpabi
Nye eke umeyeshi leke uwhetule,
Lekeya Jesus sabetanya Umeyeshi

3

Eke iye uzhe ye eke iye mumor,
Eke upadhi mu ya nwor lewa unwa Jesus,
Umanu le ulalu lobeke bu iye orbu,
Iye otogu, iye ugbor ye, leke aweji Jesus;

MH 17   Lord, In the Morning   SDAH 39
Isaac Watts, 1719 (1674-1748)
English

1
Lord, in the morning Thou shalt hear
My voice ascending high;
To Thee will I direct my prayer,
To Thee lift up mine eye.

2
Up to the hills where Christ is gone
To plead for all His saints,
Presenting at His Father's throne
Our songs and our complaints.

3
O may Thy Spirit guide my feet
In ways of righteousness;
Make every path of duty straight
And plain before my face.

4 The men that love and fear Thy name
Shall see their hopes fulfilled;
The mighty God will compass them
With favor as a shield.

MH 17   Lord, In the Morning   SDAH 39
Isaac Watts, 1719 (1674-1748)
Ekpeye Translation

1
Nye nwe ye li oyukwe
Enuji ulime ja olu,
Leka yo ma yawe edhor me,
Leka yo, ma gbabuze enye me.

2
Lo olu egbum Christ
Zhor lu dhornyi emene Aya,
Lu lorwe la agida eze
Eda orbu ye lu umekpeli ye.

3
Me mu uwa Yo dudhiga Uko me,
le ichakpa uma Ma yo,
Gbayite ichakpa gbele gbele ugboloo,
Mu chini lununu me

4
Emenem gwushegbe mu tuniyo gbe eya yo,
Uwhetugbe emezu,
Eda gbaka nazhi senigbe,
Kpormu okpulishi ulu

MH 18   Hark, thy Voice of Jesus Calling   SDAH 359

Daniel March 1868 (1816-1909)
English

1
Hark! the voice of Jesus calling,
 "Who will go and work today?
Fields are white, the harvest waiting,
Who will bear the sheaves away?"
Loud and long the Master calleth,
Rich reward He offers free;
Who will answer, gladly saying,
"Here am I, O Lord, send me"?

2
If you cannot cross the ocean.
And the heathen lands explore,
You can find the heathen nearer,
You can help them at your door;
If you cannot speak like angels,
If you cannot preach like Paul,
You can tell the love of Jesus,
 You can say He died for all.

3
If you cannot be the watchman,
Standing high on Zion's wall,
Pointing out the path to heaven,
Offering life and peace to all;
With your prayers and with your bounties
You can do what Heaven demands,
You can be like faithful Aaron,
Holding up the prophet's hands.

MH 18 Hark, thy Voice of Jesus Calling   SDAH 359
Daniel March 1868 (1816-1909)
Ekpeye Translation

1
Kpe ete luli uwhu Jesus,
Nina e-zai ugbolo tam?
Ika akadhule, ghidhi akale,
Nina ogwulorshie iye ika?
Eda olor uwhu le uwhu tutu,
ugwor bu eke bawu Ncdhi ewe,
 nna ogodhu Obu ctor musa,
Nye nwe ye, mbu me zhi mu.

2
Bule gbi iwekpodho uweshi,
Luweji ula emene ekpesu,
Ewejogbe lukpu udhor yo,
Dumagbe li unobu udhor yo,
Bule gbu ekadho kporm nyushi eso,
Bule gbu izhidho ushi uma kporm Paul,
Kaloshie ugwushi Jesus,
Ka gbu nwulu enwu lishi ye.

3
Bule gbi inwedho ike usai adhi,
Lunzo lunobudho zion
Lu utu eka lichakpa Orbioma
lunedhi budu lu uyodhu
Edhor yo lo owayi yo,
Emekpor iye orbioma wudhiga,
Ebukpor kpormu nyu uwhetu Aaron,
Lu ugbabuzie eka nye amuma

MH 18   Hark, thy Voice of Jesus Calling SDAH 359
Daniel March 1868 (1816-1909)
English

4
While the souls of men are dying,
And the Master calls for you,
Let none hear you idly saying,
 "There is nothing I can do!"
Gladly take the task He gives you,
Let His work your pleasure be;
Answer quickly when He calleth,
 "Here am I, O Lord, send me."

MH 18 Hark, thy Voice of Jesus Calling   SDAH 359
Daniel March 1868 (1816-1909)
Ekpeye Translation

4
Leke uwa umu madu dhu nwule gbe,
Mu Eda gbaka whule yo,
Ewhemu ornwu- nye nuji kpekale
"Uzhi iye, mai menidho yo",
Le ekpema etor me iye uzhi yo,
 Memu ogholo ya bu-iye etor yo,
Sashia enwa leke uwhule,
Nye nwe ye, mbu me, zhi mu.

MH 19   Chief of Sinners   SDAH 295

William McComb, (1793-1870)

English

1

Chief of sinners though I be,
Jesus shed His blood for me;
Died that I might live on high,
Died that I might never die;
As the branch is to the vine,
I am His, and He is mine.

2

O the height of Jesus' love!
Higher than the heaven above,
Deeper than the deepest sea,
Lasting as eternity;
Love that found me-wondrous thought!
Found me when I sought Him not!

3

Chief of sinners though I be,
Christ is all in all to me;
All my wants to Him are known,
All my sorrows are His own;
Safe with Him from earthly strife,
He sustains the hidden life.

MH 19   Chief of Sinners   SDAH 295
William McComb, (1793-1870)
Ekpeye Translation

1
Morbu nye ishi umeyeshi,
Jesus wosa ubala ya li me,
Unwulu meke mbe lolu,
Unwulu meke ngu nwulu
Kpe eleka zhele lushi,
Morbu aya, Ya bu ame

2
Obu eke ugwushi Jesus
Akale ulolu orbioma,
Udhu ya kale udhu olimini,
Ikashi ya gwulu orgwulu
Ugwushim uwhejor me lime iye otogu,
Wheji me leke mo wudhi ga ma.

3
Mobu nye ishi umeyeshi,
Christ bu nyi me gbele gbele iye,
Umajikpo umekpeli me,
Gbele gbele agbezhi me bu aya,
udorkpewe me lu uwudhuma uwa,
Umajikpo budu woli owoli.

MH 20   Jesus is Coming Again   SDAH 213

Jessie E. Strout (1872-)

English

1

Lift up the trumpet, and loud let it ring:
Jesus is coming again!
Cheer up, ye pilgrims, be joyful and sing:
Jesus is coming again!

Chorus
Coming again, coming again,
Jesus is coming again!

2

Echo it, hilltops; proclaim it, ye plains:
Jesus is coming again!
Coming in glory, the Lamb that was slain;
Jesus is coming again!

3

Heavings of earth, tell the vast, wondering throng:
Jesus is coming again!
Tempests and whirlwinds, the anthem prolong;
Jesus is coming again!

4

Nations are angry, by this we do know
Jesus is coming again!
Knowledge increases; men run to and fro;
Jesus is coming again!

MH 20   Jesus is Coming Again   SDAH 213
Jessie E. Strout (1872-)
Ekpeye Translation

1
Gbabuzeni ordu me ekpor ya la olu
Jesus eja gba bu udor,
Padhiwe nwu uzhi uma lo obu etor lo orbu,
Jesus eja gba bu udor

Chorus
Eja bu udor, eja bu udor,
Jesus eja gba bu udor

2
Egbu whuani uhu, ogbo iwho kalorshie ani,
Jesus eja gba bu udor,
Eja ligili, ugagam ugborgbe ogbum,
Jesus eja gba bu udor

3
Ekpor uwinwe uwa, uka ogbo iye otogu,
Jesus eja gba bu udor,
Eke uwele li ebilika, orbu etor lawa utor
Jesus eja gba bu udor

4
Umu uwa wudhugbe uma, amu ye amajikpor,
Jesus eja gba bu udor
Eke umajiye madu gbagbe, Orzu lununu
Jesus eja gba bu udor.

MH21   More Love to Thee O Christ   SDAH 458
Mrs. E. Prentiss, 1856 (1818-1878)
English

1

More love to thee, O Christ, more love to thee!
Hear thou the prayer I make on bended knee.
This is my earnest plea: More love, O Christ, to thee;
more love to thee, more love to thee!

2

Once earthly joy I craved, sought peace and rest;
now thee alone I seek, give what is best.
This all my prayer shall be: More love, O Christ, to thee;
more love to thee, more love to thee!

3

Let sorrow do its work, come grief and pain;
sweet are thy messengers, sweet their refrain,
when they can sing with me: More love, O Christ, to thee;
more love to thee, more love to thee!

4

Then shall my latest breath whisper thy praise;
this be the parting cry my heart shall raise;
this still its prayer shall be: More love, O Christ, to thee;
more love to thee, more love to thee!

MH 21   More Love to Thee O Christ   SDAH458
Mrs. E. Prentiss, 1856 (1818-1878)
Ekpeye Translation

1

Mor gwushi Yo, O Christ, moi gwushi Yo,
Nuji edhor mordhu dhor, lu kpunuko me,
Ombu egedhe edhor me, Mor gwushi Yo, O Christ,
Mor gwushi Yo, mor gwushi Yo.

2

Mo wudhiga etor uwa, uyodhu lu udeli,
Lu umorm mo wudhiga kwa Yo, Nem iye ka,
Om bu gbele gbele edhor me, Mor gwushi Yo, O Christ,
Mor gwushi Yo, mor gwushi Yo.

3

Agbezhi mai ugbolo ya, Akwukwa le elidhe,
Etor emene uzhi ya, Etor orbu gbe,
Eke ugwu Keju gbeme, Mor gwushi Yo, O Christ,
Mor gwushi Yo, Mor gwushi Yo

4

Padhiwe Yo, om bu ugwulu ekwa me,
Obu me kwa, om bu edhor mordhor,
Mor gwushi yo, O Christ,
Mor gwushi yo, mor gwushi yo

MH 22   More About Jesus   SDAH 245
Eliza E. Hewitt, 1887 (1851-1920)
English

1
More about Jesus, I would know,
More of His grace to others show;
More of His saving fullness see,
More of His love who died for me.

Chorus
More, more about Jesus,
More, more about Jesus;
More of His saving fullness see,
More of His love who died for me.

2
More about Jesus, let me learn,
More of His holy will discern;
Spirit of God, my teacher be,
Showing the things of Christ to me.

3
More about Jesus, in His word,
Holding communion with my Lord;
Hearing His voice in every line,
Making each faithful saying mine.

4
More about Jesus, on His throne,
Riches in glory all His own;
More of His kingdom's sure increase,
More of His coming, Prince of Peace.

MH 22   More About Jesus   SDAH 245
Eliza E. Hewitt, 1887 (1851-1920)
Ekpeye Translation

1
Ma amajo bu iye kpani Jesus,
Mu udemene wejigbe. Iyeoma ya,
Udorkpewe Ya uzuke,
lishi ugwushi, Mu unwulor li me

Chorus
Ogbo udiye kpani Jesus
Ogbo udiye kpani Jesus
Udorkpewe ya uzuke,
Lishi ugwushi mu nwulor li me

2
Mor mudhi iye kpani Jesus
Likpu echiche egwele ya zhile,
Uwuma Nye nwe ye Zhimu iye,
Tugorshi me iye kpani Jesus

3
Iye kpani Jesus lu unuka Ya,
Gbidhi umegbedhe me li
Nye-nwe-ye, mor nuji uli Ya gbele gbele ichakpa,
Umai mu nyu uwhetu ka gbu ubu aya

4
Iye kpani Jesus la agida Eze Ya,
Eze li igili bu Aya,
Ele eze ya ututu ogbo,
Ujeja ya kporm unwo eze uyodhu;

MH 23   O Jesus I Have Promised   SDAH 331

John E. Bode, 1866 (1816-1874)

English

1

O Jesus, I have promised
to serve thee to the end;
be thou forever near me,
my Master and my friend.
I shall not fear the battle
if thou art by my side,
nor wander from the pathway
if thou wilt be my guide.

2

O let me feel thee near me!
The world is ever near;
I see the sights that dazzle,
the tempting sounds I hear;
my foes are ever near me,
around me and within;
but Jesus, draw thou nearer,
and shield my soul from sin.

3

O Jesus, thou hast promised
to all who follow thee
that where thou art in glory
there shall thy servant be.
And Jesus, I have promised
to serve thee to the end;
O give me grace to follow,
my Master and my Friend.

MH 23   O Jesus I Have Promised   SDAH 331
John E. Bode, 1866 (1816-1874)
Ekpeye Translation

1
Jesus morgulem egba,
Lume ugbolo Yo,
Bule gbizhi me leli,
Edanwudho li nwuje me,
Ndeke motunye mu ulu,
bule gbizhi lu ukwu me
Mgba maliem li ichakpa Yo,
bule bu idu me.

2
Mai mmaji gbezhi ukwu me
Uwa zhi luzedhu, maim
Nweji unwudhu le nye,
Lunuji ekpor umama,
Nyegba zheli uzedhu me
Eshikoshi leme;
Jesus ja dhomu uzedhu,
Dor uwa me lumeye.

3.
Jesus Ye gwushile egba,
Le emene so gba Yo,
Gbu adhi mu izhe lu padhi
Abadhi emene Yo ezhigbe
Jesus morgulem egba,
Lumai ugbolo Yo,
Nemu ortizhi lu so Yo,
Edanwudhor li nwuje me.

MH 24   Lord I'm Coming Home SDAH 296
William J. Kirkpatrick, 1902 (1838-1921)

English

1
I've wandered far away from God,
Now I'm coming home;
The paths of sin too long I've trod;
Lord, I'm coming home.

Chorus
Coming home, coming home,
Never more to roam;
Open wide Thine arms of love;
Lord I'm coming home.

2
I've wasted many precious years,
Now I'm coming home;
I now repent with bitter tears;
Lord, I'm coming home.

3
I'm tired of sin and straying Lord,
Now I'm coming home;
I'll trust thy love believe thy word;
Lord I'm coming home.

4
My only hope, my only plea,
Now I'm coming home;
That Jesus died, and died for me;
Lord I'm coming home.

MH 24   Lord I'm Coming Home SDAH 296
William J. Kirkpatrick, 1902 (1838-1921)
Ekpeye Translation
1
Magba malilem leli Eblikpabi,
lumorm, ma yalem udhor,
Ichakpa utor umeye magba—malior,
Nye nwe ye, ma yalem udhor,
Chorus
Ma yalemu udhor, Ma yalemu udhor
Ndeke ma ladhem orzu,
Lemanyi mu eka ugwushi
Nye nwe ye ma yale mu udhor,

2
Ma tashilemu aluma tu ogbo
Lumorm mayalemu udhor
Moyosalilem lishigili ekwa
Nye nwe ye, mayalemu udhor;
3
Umeye li ukpega oyuleme,
Lumorm mayalemu udhor,
Me ewhetu ugwushi li unuka Yo,
Nye nwe ye, mayalemu udhor,

4
Unye enye me li edhor me,
Lumorm mayalemu udhor,
Jesus nwulu, nwulu lishi me
Nye nwe ye mayalemu udhor.

MH 24   Lord I'm Coming Home SDAH 296
William J. Kirkpatrick, 1902 (1838-1921)
English

5
I need His cleansing blood I know,
Now I'm coming home;
O wash me whiter than the snow;
Lord I'm coming home.

MH 24   Lord I'm Coming Home SDAH 296
William J. Kirkpatrick, 1902 (1838-1921)
 Ekpeye Translation

5
Nemu ubala Ya sawiye mamajo,
Lumorm ma yalemu udhor,
Sama mu ka mini okpor
Eligwe, Nye nwe ye, mayalemu udhor;

MH 25 How Sweet the Name of Jesus SDAH 238

John Newton, 1779 (1725-1807)

English

1
How sweet the name of Jesus sounds
In a believer's ear!
It soothes his sorrows, heals his wounds,
And drives away his fear.

2
It makes the wounded spirit whole,
And calms the troubled breast;
"Tis manna to the hungry soul,
And to the weary, rest.

3
Dear name, the rock on which I build,
My shield and hiding place,
My never failing treasury, filled
With boundless stores of grace.

4
Jesus! my Shepherd, Guardian, Friend,
My Prophet, Priest, and King!
My Lord, my life, my way, my end!
Accept the praise I bring.

5
Weak is the effort of my heart,
And cold my warmest thought;
But when I see Thee as Thou art,
I'll praise Thee as I ought.

MH 25 How Sweet the Name of Jesus SDAH 238
John Newton, 1779 (1725-1807)
Ekpeye Translation

1
Ndekpu etor Jesus torle
Le ete nye uwhetu,
Ugor nye agbezhi li elidhe
Uchima otogwu

2
Ume nye elidhe muzuke,
Uyodhuwe umekpeli,
Ubu ghidhi nyeke ugwunu
Lu udeli ike ugwulu

3
Ewam bu igwu mu monuzo
Kpulishi ulu ladhi
Uwoli me, Udhor orwayi mu yulu nye me,
Li ortizhi ogbo ogbo

4
Jesus nyu udu nyosoeja la amuma,
 nwuje li Eze me, Nye nwe ye,
budu lawu ugbo ogbo,
Natu ukala ma gala

5
Ugbakpo orgwulule ekpema me,
Echicheme tu ukayi
Eke mewejile kpu ezhile
Mekela yo lorbu

MH 26 Loving Shepherd of Thy Sheep SDAH 549

Jane E. Leeson (1807-1882)

English

1
Loving Shepherd of Thy sheep
Keep Thy lamb, in safety keep;
Nothing can Thy power withstand;
None can pluck me from Thy hand.

2
Loving Shepherd, ever near,
Teach Thy lamb Thy voice to hear;
Suffer not my steps to stray
From the straight and narrow way.

3
Where Thou leadest I would go,
Walking in Thy steps below,
Till within the heavenly fold
I my Shepherd shall behold.

MH 26 Loving Shepherd of Thy Sheep SDAH 549
Jane E. Leeson (1807-1882)
Ekpeye Translation

1
Nye ugwushi u-du ugaga,
Mojiketu ornor Yo,
Uzhiye onuzo nyidho
ugbakpo Yo, uzhe iye
Ogonu dhome leka Yo.

2
Nye ugwushi udu ugaga, zhili uzedhu,
Zhi ornor Yo munuji uli Yo,
Ewhemu edanuko me gaye
Lichakpa mu edenyu udem.

3
Adhi iduleme bu adhi meze,
Lu ukaze le edanuko Yo,
Dhuma eke orbioma whule
Me nye enye li nyu udu ugaga.

MH 27 King of Glory, King of Peace   SDAH 243
George Herbert (1593-1633

English

1
King of glory, King of peace, I will love Thee;
And that love may never cease, I will move Thee.
Thou hast granted my request, Thou hast heard me;
Thou didst note my working breast, Thou hast spared me.
2
Wherefore with my utmost art I will sing Thee,
And the cream of all my heart I will bring Thee.
Though my sins against me cried, Thou didst clear me;
And alone, when they replied, Thou didst hear me.
3
Seven whole days, not one in seven, I will raise Thee;
In my heart, though not in heaven I can raise Thee.
Small it is, in this poor sort to enroll Thee:
Even eternity's too short to extol Thee.

MH 27 King of Glory, King of Peace   SDAH 243
George Herbert (1593-1633
Ekpeye Translation

1
Eze igili le Eze uyodhu, Mer gwushi Yo,
Ugwushi mu orgwulo orgwulu, Mo onu ma Yo,
Ye ewhenyi leme edhor me, Ye enuji nyile me,
Ye enatule ugbolo me, Ye edor leme,
2
Lekpor li eke uli etor me, Mor gwuni Yo,
Le gbele gbele etor ekpema me, ma gala nyi Yo,
Umeyeshi me emegidhe, leme, Ye cgwor le me,
Leke ghe neten sagbe, Ye nujin le me
3
Ogbo eye isabor budho ne eye, ma padhiwe Yo
Lekpema me izhe le orbioma, ma gbabuze Yo
Uzhi ntuko lime uji uyam lu ugbashi ewa yo
Etor orbioma zhi ntukor Lu ugbabuze ewa Yo.

MH28   Work for the Night is Coming SDAH 375

Mrs. Anna L. Coghill, 1854 (1836-1907)
Ekpeye Translation

1
Work for the night is coming,
Work through the morning hours;
Work while the dew is sparkling;
Work 'mid springing flowers.
Work when the day grows brighter,
Work in the glowing sun;
Work for the night is coming,
When man's work is done.
2
Work for the night is coming,
Work thro' the sunny noon;
Fill brightest hours with labor,
Rest comes sure and soon.
Give every flying minute
Something to keep in store;
Work for the night is coming,
When man works no more.

3
Work for the night is coming,
Under the sunset skies;
While their bright tints are glowing,
Work for daylight flies.
Work till the last beam fadeth,
Fadeth to shine no more;
Work while the night is dark'ning,
When man's work is o'er.

MH28   Work for the Night is Coming SDAH 375
Mrs. Anna L. Coghill, 1854 (1836-1907)
Ekpeye Translation

1
Ugbolo abali zhi lu uja,
Metu ugbolo lo oyukwe,
Mai ekemu igiligi dhu zhor,
eke ushi zhilu umaigbe,
Mai ekemu eye zhi gedhe,
lu ukpudhu elanwu uma,
ugbolo abali zhi lu uja,
Lu ugwulu ugbolo madu.

2
Ugbolo abali zhi lu uja,
Mai eke elanwu dhu umu
Mai eke ugbolo lekele uma,
Ude-eli zhi lu uja enwa,
Nai gbele gbele ugbe iye ugbeke,
Mu ugbeke li ime udhor,
Ugbolo abali zhi lu uja,
Leke madu eme dho dhe.

3
Ugbolo abali zhi lu uja,
Lu ukpudhu uda elanwu olu,
mai ekemu, unwumali eye zhi gedhor,
Mai iyedor eye dhuga,
Mai dhuma ugwulu elanwu ela,
Ugwulu ulor dhu udor,
Ugbolo Nye nwe ye zhi lu uja,
Eke ugbolo madu gwulule.

MH 29 Bringing In the Sheaves SDAH 369
Knowles Shaw (1834-1878)

English

1
Sowing in the morning, sowing seeds of kindness,
Sowing in the noontide and the dewy eve,
Waiting for the harvest and the time of reaping –
We shall come rejoicing, bringing in the sheaves.

Chorus
Bringing in the sheaves, bringing in the sheaves,
We shall come rejoicing, bringing in the sheaves.
Bringing in the sheaves, bringing in the sheaves,
We shall come rejoicing, bringing in the sheaves.

2
Sowing in the sunshine, sowing in the shadows,
Fearing neither clouds nor winter's chilling breeze;
By and by the harvest and the labor ended –
We shall come rejoicing, bringing in the sheaves.

3
Going forth with weeping, sowing for the Master,
Tho the loss sustained our spirit often grieves;
When our weeping's over He will bid us welcome –
We shall come rejoicing, bringing in the sheaves

MH 29 Bringing In the Sheaves SDAH 369
Knowles Shaw (1834-1878)
Ekpeye Translation

1

Kpashi lime oyukwe, Kpashi ukpushi egwuma,
Kpashi lime echie eye, lu uda igi-ligi,
Seji mu iye kadhu, Leke ugwulorshie iye ika,
Ye ya ja lu obu etor; Lugala iye ika

Chorus
Lugala iye ika, Lugala iye ika,
Ye ya ja lu obu etor, Lugala iye ika,
Lugala iye ika, Lugala iye ika,
Ye ya ja lu obu etor, Lugala iye ika

2

Kpashi li umu elanwu, Kpashi li adhi uyodhu
Etunye igiligi lu uwele Okidhika,
 Emekpor mu iye kadhu le, Leke ugbolo gwulu le,
Ye ya ja lu obu etor, lugala iye ika

3

Lu kpashi lishigili ekwa, Lu kpashini Eda nwu udhor ye
Iyemu wuluu nyor ye, dheyedhe lo obu
Eke ekwa gakpole, mu ukani ye ejalenyi,
Ye ya ja lu obu ctor, lugala iye ika

MH 30   Now the Day is Over   SDAH 52

Mary A. Lathbury, 1877 (1841-1913)

English

1
Now the day is over,
night is drawing nigh,
Shadows of the evening
steal across the sky.

2
Father, give the weary,
calm and sweet repose;
With Thy tenderest blessing
May our eyelids close.

3
Through the long night
watches,
may thine angels spread
Their white wings above me,
watching round my bed.

MH 30   Now the Day is Over   SDAH 52
Mary A. Lathbury, 1877 (1841-1913)
Ekpeye Translation

1
E-ye agamale,
Abali zhi uzedhu,
E-nye o-yi-la,
Onuzo le lo olu

2
Eda nedhe uyodhu,
Le etor unana,
Yalu uwokwanu ma Yo
Leke unyi nina

3
Eke udhumale la abali
Emene uzhi ma Yo,
Wushi gbem eyi usa magbe,
Unyeke gbe agbada me

MH 31 Peace, Perfect Peace SDAH 463
Edward H. Bickersteth, 1875 (1825-1906)
English

1
Peace, perfect peace,
in this dark world of sin?
The blood of Jesus whispers
peace within.

2
Peace, perfect peace,
by thronging duties pressed?
To do the will of Jesus:
this is rest.

3
Peace, perfect peace,
with loved ones far away?
In Jesus' keeping
we are safe, and they.

4
Peace, perfect peace,
our future all unknown?
Jesus we know, and
 He is on the throne.

MH 31   Peace, Perfect Peace   SDAH 463
Edward H. Bickersteth, 1875 (1825-1906)
Ekpeye Translation

1
Uyodhu egedhe uyodhu,
Lu uwa igileni umeshim?
Ubala Jesus taku gala uyodhu

2
Uyodhu egedhe uyodhu
Lu ume eke ugbolo?
Ume echiche Jesus
Bu ude-eli

3
Uyodhu egedhe uyodhu
Yele emene ugwushi zhi gbe lu utor,
Li Jesus, ye ligbele anwe udorkpewe

4
Uyodhu egedhe uyodhu
Iye zhi lununu ye ameje
Jesus ye amajor
zhi la agida eze

MH 32   Abide with Me   SDAH 50
Henry F. Lyte, 1847 (1793-1847)
English

1
Abide with me; fast falls the eventide;
The darkness deepens; Lord with me abide!
When other helpers fail and comforts flee,
Help of the helpless, O abide with me.

2
Swift to its close ebbs out life's little day;
Earth's joys grow dim; its glories pass away;
Change and decay in all around I see;
O Thou who changest not, abide with me.

3
I need Thy presence every passing hour.
What but Thy grace can foil the tempter's power?
Who, like Thyself, my guide and stay can be?
Through cloud and sunshine, Lord, abide with me.

4
I fear no foe, with Thee at hand to bless;
Ills have no weight and tears no bitterness.
Where is death's sting? Where, grave, thy victory?
I triumph still, if Thou abide with me!

MH 32   Abide with Me   SDAH 50
Henry F. Lyte, 1847 (1793-1847)
Ekpeye Translation

1
Nashi kejim le eke ela gale
igileni adale, Eda nazhi keijm,
Eke ushie eka nyu ushieka ezhedhe
Shini nye nwe ushieeka, nazhi kejim.

2
Ukpenwa lu ukaze, le budu eye ntukor,
Etor uwa dhu gwulu, upadhiya agamale,
Ugbanwo li udhodho bu iye mezhili unotu,
Yo nyemu agbanwo, Nashi kejim.

3
Mo wudhiga Yo, Le gbele gbele ugbe gaga,
Gama Yo lu umegbo, ugbakpo umama,
Yo kpormu Yo, Unyeke li budu me zhi
Li igiligi li elanwu, Nashi kejim.

4
Mo tunyem nye egba, Lekele iwokwani me,
Gbiyor nwe ugbakpo ekwa new ilu,
Nde ugbakpo enwu, ili nde umegbo yo?
Me emegbo bu emegbo la-I nazhi kejileme.

MH33 ... Praise, My Soul the King of Heaven
..SDAH 4
Henry Francis Lyte (1793-1847)
English

1
Praise, my soul, the King of heaven;
To his feet thy tribute bring;
Ransomed, healed, restored, forgiven,
Who like thee His praise should sing?
Praise Him, praise Him, alleluia!
Praise the everlasting King.

2
Praise him for his grace and favor
To our fathers in distress;
Praise him still the same forever,
Slow to chide and swift to bless:
Praise Him, praise Him, alleluia!
Glorious in His faithfulness.

3
Tenderly He shields and spares us;
Well our feeble frame he knows;
In his hands He gently bears us,
Rescues us from all our foes.
Praise Him, praise Him, alleluia!
Widely yet his mercy flows.

4
Angels, help us to adore him;
Ye behold him face to face;
Sun and moon, bow down before him,
Dwellers all in time and space.
Praise Him, praise Him, alleluia!
Praise with us the God of grace.

MH33 Praise, My Soul the King of Heaven .SDAH 4
Henry Francis Lyte (1793-1847)
Ekpeye Translation

1
Uwame padhiwe eze Orbioma,
Lu uko Ya, galanya upadhi,
Ugo, ugwo, unedhi ortizhi,
Nina ukelaya ezhi kpe?
Padhiwa, Padhiwa,
Padhiwa, Padhiwa,
Padhiwe eze orbioma.

2
Padhiwa le ortizhi le egwu ma Ya,
Une emene eda ye la akwukwu,
Padhiwe dha kpormu awu unuzu uwudhor eke uma
Uwokwani enwe enwa
Padhiwa, Padhiwa, Padhiwa
Padhiwa, padhiwe eze orbioma.
3
Le eka uma udor ye awu nweke ye
Umajikpo kpuye azhile
Lime eka Ya moji keye
Udorkpewe ye leka nwe egba;
Padhiwa, padhiwa,
Padhiwa, padhiwa, kpermu ortizhi Ye Zukpor.
4
Emene uzhi uma, Kpeni kejini ye,
Iwejani upi lu upi,
Elanwu li ema kpornya nyi ishi le ele,
Gbele gbele emenem begbe lu uwa,
Padhiwa, padhiwa, Padhiwa, padhiwa
Padhiwe Eblikpabi Ortizhi.

MH34   Immortal Invisible God Only Wise   SDAH 21

Walter Chalmers Smith, 1867 (1824-1908)
English

1
Immortal, invisible, God only wise,
In light inaccessible hid from our eyes,
Most blessed, most glorious, the Ancient of
Days,
Almighty, victorious, Thy great Name we
praise.

2
Unresting, unhasting, and silent as light,
Nor wanting, nor wasting, Thou rulest in might;
Thy justice, like mountains, high soaring above
Thy clouds, which are fountains of goodness
and love.
3
To all, life Thou givest, to both great and small;
In all life Thou livest, the true life of all;
We blossom and flourish as leaves on the tree,
And wither and perish – but naught changeth
Thee.
4
Great Father of glory, pure Father of light,
Thine angels adore Thee, all veiling their sight;
All praise we would render; O help us to see
'Tis only the splendor of light hideth Thee!

MH34   Immortal Invisible God Only Wise   SDAH 21

Walter Chalmers Smith, 1867 (1824-1908)
Ekpeye Translation

1
Unwulu ormwulu, unwe uweji enye
Eblikpabi neten maji Iye,
Lu usamali, unwe ugwugbedhe,
uwoli li ekpeleni ye
Uwokwani kakpo ligbc, igili kakpoligbe, nye zhi lukani
Nye eke ugbakpo, ewa Yo yu apadhiwe

2
Unwe udeli, unwe umeshi enwa, uyodhu
Kpormu asa-uwe, Unwe uwudhiga unwe utashi,
 i-chi lu ugbakpo ukwunu uma Yo,
Kpormu egbu, ulonyi ma eke olu, igiligi Yo,
Bu mini gbalorshie, umali ugwushi

3
Gbele gbele budu, inedhi nye obu eke linye ntuko.
Gbele gbele budu, ibedhi, gbele gbele budu uma,
Ye ya azordhu mu awanahor, kpormu uwhor ushi lu ushi,
Mu ayaweli mu agwulor; Iye iye gbanwo Yo.

4
Eke Eda, ebube, Eda uma usamali
Emene ushi uma, kpeni gbe, Yo wokegbe upi gbe,
Gbele gbele upadhi, ye agala shi shi, eka mu anotu,
bu kwa egedhe, usamali, bu iye woke Yo.

MH 35   O Worship the King   SDAH 83

Robert Grant, 1833 (1779-1838)

English

1

O worship the King, all glorious above,
O gratefully sing His wonderful love;
Our Shield and Defender, the Ancient of Days,
Pavilioned in splendor, and girded with praise.

2

O tell of His might, O sing of His grace,
Whose robe is the light, whose canopy space,
His chariots of wrath the deep thunderclouds form,
And dark is His path on the wings of the storm.

3

Thy bountiful care, what tongue can recite?
It breathes in the air, it shines in the light;
It streams from the hills, it descends to the plain,
And sweetly distills in the dew and the rain.

4

Frail children of dust, and feeble as frail,
In Thee do we trust, nor find Thee to fail;
Thy mercies how tender, how firm to the end!
Our Maker, Defender, Redeemer, and Friend.

MH 35   O Worship the King   SDAH 83
Robert Grant, 1833 (1779-1838)
Ekpeye Translation

1

Ja akpeni nyi Eze, lgigili zhi lo olu,
Gonu orbu etor, lu uka ugwushi Ya,
Okpulishi ulu, li nye udu ulu, nye zhi lu ukani,
Adhi uwoli zorzor, Zuke lu upadhi

2

Kanyi ugbakpo Ya, gwu orbu ortizhi Ya
Usamali bu kapa Ya, Orbioma kpupi dhia,
Ughor uwudhuma Ya, Bu eke igiligi ama,
Igeleni bu ichakpa Ya le eyi eke uwele.

3

Eke unyeke Ya, eli Idho akalorshie?
Usekeli lu uwukayi unwulorshie li usamali,
Ugbalorshi le olu egbu gbala ele zorzor
Nwagbali li igiligi li mini dede.

4

Umeledhe uya kpuegbe uza, dagbe uya kpormu uya,
Li Yo yagbai uwa, ndeke enagbo ye,
Obu eke ortizhi Yo, mojike dhuma ugbo-gbo,
Nyor kpu ye, nyu ulu ye, nyu ugawe ye li nwuje.

MH 36   All Things Bright and Beautiful   SDAH
93

Cecil F. Alexander, 1848 (1818-1895)
English

1
All things bright and beautiful
All creatures great and small
All things wise and wonderful
The Lord God made them all.
2
Each little flow'r that opens
Each little bird that sings
He made their glowing colours
He made their tiny wings.
3
The purple-headed mountain
The river running by
The sunset and the morning
That brighten up the sky.
4
The cold wind in the winter
The pleasant summer sun
The ripe fruits in the garden
He made them, every one.
5
He gave us eyes to see them
And lips that we might tell
How great is God Almighty
Who has made all things well.

MH 36   All Things Bright and Beautiful   SDAH 93
Cecil F. Alexander, 1848 (1818-1895)
Ekpeye Translation

1
Gbele gbele iye zorgbe orzorzor,
Awu bu eke lawu ntukor,
Gbele gbele iye majigbe eke iye,
Eblikpabi kpukpo gbe

2
Falawa ntukom sagor
Unu ntukorm gwor orbum,
Ya mai agba umam agbe
Ya mai eyi ntukorm agbe.

3
Eke egbu mu bukonyor,
Oliminim gbalagbor,
Elanwu ela lawu oyukwe,
Amu nwuma liwor olu.

4
Ukayi uwele okidhika,
Elanwu umam ulamini,
Ukpulushi saagbe li ika
Ya mekpo gbele gbele gbe.

5
Ya ne ye ekpeleni ma weji gbe,
Ya ne ye ugbanu ukalorshie,
Ndekpu obu-eke Eblikpabi zhile,
Nyem mekpor gbele gbele iye.

MH 37   God Will Take Care of You   SDAH 99
Civilla D. Martin (1866-1948)
English

1
Be not dismayed whate'er betide,
God will take care of you;
beneath his wings of love abide,
God will take care of you.

Chorus
God will take care of you,
through every day, o'er all the way;
he will take care of you,
God will take care of you.

2
Through days of toil when heart doth fail,
God will take care of you;
when dangers fierce your path assail,
God will take care of you.

3
All you may need he will provide,
God will take care of you;
nothing you ask will be denied,
God will take care of you.

4
No matter what may be the test,
God will take care of you;
lean, weary one, upon his breast,
God will take care of you

MH 37   God Will Take Care of You   SDAH 99

Civilla D. Martin (1866-1948)

Ekpeye Translation

1
Egba agbezhi le iye kpani yo,
Eblikpabi enye ke yo,
Lu ukpudhu eyi ya ugwushi zhi,
Eblikpabi enye ke yo,

Chorus
Eblikpabi enye ke yo,
Le gbele gbele, eye, gbele gbele ichakpa,
Ya enye-ke-yo,
Eblikapbi enye ke yo

2
Le eye akwukwu, leke ekpema yo dale,
Eblikpabi enye ke yo
Eke iye otogu yebini le ichakpa yo
Eblikpabi enye ke yo;

3
Iye iwudhigale enekpo yo,
Eblikpabi enye key o
Iye idhor le, ndeke akwa yo,
Eblikpabi enye ke yo

4
Kpu umama uwa, ukelike,
Eblikpabi enye ke yo,
Nye eyi kali, dabenyi li ya
Eblikpabi enya ke yo,

MH 38 God Moves in a Mysterious Way SDAH 107
William Cowper (1731-1800)

English

1
God moves in a mysterious way
His wonders to perform;
He plants His footsteps in the sea,
And rides upon the storm.

2
Ye fearful saints, fresh courage take;
The clouds ye so much dread
Are big with mercy, and shall break
In blessings on your head.

3
Judge not the Lord by feeble sense,
But trust Him for His grace;
Behind a frowning providence
He hides a smiling face.

4
His purposes will ripen fast,
Unfolding every hour;
The bud may have a bitter taste,
But sweet will be the flower.

5
Blind unbelief is sure to err,
And scan His work in vain;
God is His own interpreter,
And He will make it plain.

MH 38 God Moves in a Mysterious Way SDAH 107
William Cowper (1731-1800)
Ekpeye Translation

1
Ichakpa Eblikpabi zhi igili
Iye unyodhenye bu iye ume
Uzorshi uko ya le olimini
Ugadhiga le eke uwele.

2
Emene uzhi uma otogu, Kayiteni uma
uwu,
Li igiligi mu itunye-nyi
Eke ortizhi li uwokwani,
Agala lishi yo.

3
Ekpe Eblikpabi ikpe umajiye
Dabeni lor ortizhi Ya,
Lu ukwudhu iye uwudhuma Orbioma,
uwuke iye umudhie umu.

4
Echiche Ya meshi enwa enwa
Ulor gbele gbele ekele
Ina ya enwe etor nwilu
Anwu ya orto bu etor.

Nye nwe uwhetu ador bu ikpe,
Lu ugwe ugbeweji ugbolo ya,
Eblikpabi kalorshie- tu iye,
Umea mu uwo enwe.

MH 39   When I Survey the Wondrous Cross
SDAH 154

Isaac watts, 1719 (1674-1748)

English

1

When I survey the wondrous cross
on which the Prince of Glory died;
my richest gain I count but loss,
and pour contempt on all my pride.

2

Forbid it, Lord, that I should boast,
save in the death of Christ, my God;
all the vain things that charm me most,
I sacrifice them to his blood.

3

See, from his head, his hands, his feet,
sorrow and love flow mingled down.
Did e'er such love and sorrow meet,
or thorns compose so rich a crown.

4

Were the whole realm of nature mine,
that were an offering far too small;
love so amazing, so divine,
demands my soul, my life, my all.

MH 39   When I Survey the Wondrous Cross
SDAH 154

Isaac watts, 1719 (1674-1748)
Ekpeye Translation

1
Eke mortor ushi uye lu uka
Adhi Akpana Eze igili nwulu,
Iye eke ibalame tadhu ewe
Me enye dakpolem, ideme ele

2
Eblikpabi ewhe mu edide
Gama le enwu mu Christ, Nye Nwe
me, Ogbo iye enwe ibala, tor me etor,
Morsor wa eja lubala Ya.

3
Nyetu li ishi, li eka, li uko,
agbezhi lu ugwushi wuda legbe
Uji- ugwushim la agbezhi ezhile,
Iye ugwu onyole okpulishi eze.

4
Kpormu iye orbioma bukpor hor ame,
Yabu iye uke zhi kwa ntuko
Ugwushi unyodhenye leke egwele
Wudhiga uwa me, li gbele gbele iye
me.

MH 40 Ride On in Majesty SDAH 160
Henry H. Milman, 1827 (1719-1868)
English

1
Ride on! ride on in majesty!
Hark, all the tribes hosanna cry;
O Savior meek, pursue Thy road
With palms and scattered garments strowed.

2
Ride on! ride on in majesty!
In lowly pomp ride on to die;
O Christ, Thy triumphs now begin
O'er captive death and conquered sin.

3
Ride on! ride on in majesty!
The winged squadrons of the sky
Look down with sad and wondering eyes
To see the approaching sacrifice.

4
Ride on! ride on in majesty!
In lowly pomp ride on to die;
Bow Thy meek head to mortal pain,
Then take, O God, Thy power and reign.

MH 40 Ride On in Majesty SDAH 160
Henry H. Milman, 1827 (1719-1868)
Ekpeye Translation

1
Gbaze, gbaze, eze ugbakpo
Kpete li iye gbelebele igbu kagbe,
Nyu gawe ye kaze ichakpa Yo,
Le ormu li kapa ugbashi gbe.

2
Gbaze, gbaze, eze ugbakpo
Li ide, gbaze keii enwu,
Christ, ize ugo Yo odhu male
lu umegbo enwu lu umeyeshi.

3
Gbaze, gbaze, eze ugbakpo
Eyi emene ulu zhigbe lo olu
Nyeshi La agbeshi li unwodhu enye,
Lu unotu ujeja orseja.

4
Gbaze, gbaze, eze ugbakpo
Li ide gbaze keji enwu,
Gbadawe ishi Yo lelidhe madu,
Eblikpabi gonu ugbakpo Yo michi.

MH 41 Before Jehovah's Awful Throne SDAH 82
Isaac Watts, 1719 (1674-1748)
English

1

Before Jehovah's awful throne,
Ye nations, bow with sacred joy;
Know that the Lord is God alone;
He can create, and He destroy.

2

His sovereign power, without our aid,
Made us of clay, and formed us men;
and when like wandering sheep we strayed,
He brought us to His fold again.

3

We'll crowd His gates with thankful songs,
High as the heavens our voices raise;
And earth, with her ten thousand tongues,
Shall fill His courts with sounding praise.

4

Wide as the world is His command,
Vast as Eternity His love;
Firm as a rock His truth shall stand,
When rolling years shall cease to move.

MH 41 Before Jehovah's Awful Throne SDAH 82
Isaac Watts, 1719 (1674-1748)
Ekpeye Translation

1
Lununu agida eze Eblikpabi,
Eluwa gbadagbe ishi ele lo obu etor,
Lumaji Ebilikpabi, neten bu Nye nwe ye,
Ya bu nye orkpu awu tashi.

2
Ugbakpo eze ma Ya eka ye zhela,
Ugodhu uza mu kpuwe ye madu,
Kpormu ugaga, ye akpawulor,
Ugonugba ye logbo Ya udor.

3
Ye agbagboni le agbeleta, lo obu etor,
Uli ye la olu kpormu orbioma,
Eluwa lunu kwulu unu idho gbe,
Oyulu ka-gbe leke upadhi.

4
Utu uka Ya bu-eke kpormu uwa,
Ugwushi gwulu orgwulu, uzhegani kpormu igwu,
Ishishi uka ya nuzo
Leke ugbadhe ala useji le.

MH 42   Jesus Loves Me   SDAH 190

Anna B. Warner (1820-1915)

English

1
Jesus loves me! this I know,
For the Bible tells me so;
Little ones to Him belong
They are weak but He is strong

Chorus
Yes, Jesus loves me!
Yes, Jesus loves me!
Yes, Jesus loves me!
The Bible tells me so.

2
Jesus loves me! He who died
Heaven's gate to open wide:
He will wash away my sin,
Let His little child come in.

3
Jesus, take this heart of mine,
Make it pure and wholly thine;
On the cross You died for me,
I will love and live for Thee.

MH 42   Jesus Loves Me   SDAH 190

Anna B. Warner (1820-1915)

Ekpeye Translation

1
Jesus gwushi me! Ma maji kpe
Ukpalahu egwele kani me kpe,
Umeledhe bu gbe aya, Udagbe uya,
Ya we nwe ugbakpo

Chorus
Legedhe Jesus ugwushi me,
Legedhe Jesus gwushi me,
Legedhe Jesus gwushi me
Ukpalahu egwele kani me kpe

2
Jesus gwushi me, Nye mu nwulor,
Egbeleta orbioma gwudhi egbe,
Asamakpo umeyeshi me,
Unwo ntukor Ya kpudhu.

3
Jesus gonu ekpema me
Me mu uzor mu buhor ayo
Lu ushi uye lu uka enwulu nyo me,
Mor gwushi am mbe nyi yo

MH 43   Rejoice, the Lord Is King   SDAH 221
Charles Wesley (1707-1788)
English

1
Rejoice, the Lord is King! Your Lord and King adore!
Rejoice, give thanks, and sing and triumph evermore
Lift up your heart, lift up your voice!
Rejoice, again I say, rejoice!

2
Jesus, the Savior, reigns, The God of truth and love;
When He had purged our stains, He took His seat
above
Lift up your heart, lift up your voice!
Rejoice, again I say, rejoice!

3
His kingdom cannot fail, He rules o'er earth and
heaven
The keys of death and grave Are to our Jesus given
Lift up your heart, lift up your voice!
Rejoice, again I say, rejoice!

4
Rejoice in glorious hope! Our Lord the judge shall
come,
And take His servants up to their eternal home
Lift up your heart, lift up your voice!
Rejoice, again I say, rejoice!

MH 43   Rejoice, the Lord Is King   SDAH 221
Charles Wesley (1707-1788)
Ekpeye Translation

1

Padhi Nye nwe ye bu Eze, Kpeni Nye nwe ye li Eze yo,
Padhi, kela li orbu lugo, Gbele gbele gbele ekele,
Gbabuze ekpema li uli yo,
Padhigba udor, maaka, padhi

2

Jesus, Nyu gawe ye echi,
Eblikpabi ishishuka lu ugwushi Ekemu,
Anamakpo umeshi ye,
Ugonu unashi li orbioma,
Gbabuze ekpema li uli yo,
Padhigba udor, ma-aka padhi

3

Ndeke ele-Eze ya ada, Uchi gbedhe eluwa li orbioma,
Sapi enwu lawu ili, negbe Jesus le eka,
Gbabuze ekpema li uli yo,
Padhigba udor, ma-aka, Padhi!

4

Padhi li igili unye enye! Nye nwe ye li Nyi ikpe dhuja,
Alawor emene ushi ya olu,
Lu udhor budu orgwulu orgwulu,
Gbabuze ekpema li uli yo,
Padhigba udor ma-aka padhi.

MH 44   Jesus Shall Reign   SDAH 227

Isaac Watts, 1719 (1674-1748)

English

1
Jesus shall reign where'er the sun
Does his successive journeys run;
His kingdom stretch from shore to shore,
Till moons shall wax and wane no more.

2
People and realms of ev'ry tongue
Dwell on His love with sweetest song,
And infant voices shall proclaim
Their early blessings on His name.

3
Blessings abound wherever He reigns;
The prisoner leaps to lose his chains;
The weary find eternal rest,
And all who suffer want are blessed.

4
Let every creature rise and bring
Honors peculiar to our King;
Angels descend with songs again,
And earth repeat the loud amen!

MH 44   Jesus Shall Reign   SDAH 227

Isaac Watts, 1719 (1674-1748)

Ekpeye Translation

1
Jesus echi la adhi elanwu zhi,
Umegbo ya kaze ununu,
Eleze Ya godhu lunoshi dhuma unoshi,
Dhuma eke esema gwehor nwumali

2
Emene hegbe li gbele gbele adhi,
Ubegbe lu ugwushi Ya li orbu etor,
Uli umeledhe, akalorshie legbe,
Uwokwanni, uwa nwegbe lewa ya

3
Uwokwani zuke la adhi, uchile,
Emene ikoli padhigbe lu unama gbe,
Nyu ugbakpo dale,
Weji budu ogbo ogbo
Uwokwani emene, wudhigagbe iye
uma.

4
Gbele gbele iye ukpugbe lai,
Migala, Odhu-esor kibe mi Eze ye,
Emene uzhi uma jagbe luli orbu udor
Eluwa chi ikpu udor, gbu uzhikpe

MH 45   All Hail the Power of Jesus' Name SDAH 229

Edward Perronet, 1779 (1726-1792)

English

1

All hail the power of Jesus' name! Let angels prostrate fall;
Bring forth the royal diadem, and crown Him Lord of all.
Bring forth the royal diadem, and crown Him Lord of all.

2

Ye chosen seed of Israel's race, ye ransomed from the fall,
Hail Him who saves you by His grace, and crown Him Lord of all.
Hail Him who saves you by His grace, and crown Him Lord of all.

Let every kindred, every tribe on this terrestrial ball
To Him all majesty ascribe, and crown Him Lord of all.
To Him all majesty ascribe, and crown Him Lord of all.

4

O that with yonder angel throng we at His feet may fall!
We'll join the everlasting song, and crown Him Lord of all.
We'll join the everlasting song, and crown Him Lord of all.

MH 45 All Hail the Power of Jesus' Name SDAH 229

Edward Perronet, 1779 (1726-1792)

Ekpeye Translation

1
Gbele gbele iye ka, ugbakpo ewa Jesus,
Emene uzhi uma dagbe lele,
Gala okpulushi eze ugbakpo,
Mime wani Eze kakpoligbe,
Gala okpulushi eze ugbakpo,
Mime wami Eze kakpoligbe

2
Yai emene Isrealim ulorto gbe,
Yai emenem udorgbo lu udada,
Padhiwe nyor dor yo lor ortizhi,
Mime wani Eze kakpoligbe,
Padhiwe nyor dor yo lor ortizhi,
Mime wani eze kakpoligbe.

3
Gbele gbele madu li, Gbele gbele unu ekpor,
Lu uwa mu ushikoshom,
Ya bu nyu unedgbe gbele gbele ugbakpo,
Mewe ani Eze kakpoligbe,
Ya bu nyu unegbe gbele gbele ugbakpo,
Mewe ani Eze kakpoligbe.

4
Ligbum emene uyodhu nazhor gbe, Ya ada li uko Ya,
Dhunyi migwuni orbu ogbo ogbo,
Mime wani Eze kakpoligbe,
Ogbo ogbo mime wani eze kakpoligbe.

MH 46 All Glory, Laud, and Honor.SDAH 230

Theophilus of Orleans (750-821)
Tr. By John M. Neale (1818-1866)

English

1

All glory, laud, and honor,
to thee, Redeemer, King,
to whom the lips of children
made sweet hosannas ring.
Thou art the King of Israel,
thou David's royal Son,
who in the Lord's name comest,
the King and Blessed One.

2

The company of angels
are praising thee on high,
and we with all creation
in chorus make reply.
The people of the Hebrews
with psalms before thee went;
our prayer and praise and anthems
before thee we present.

3

To thee, before thy passion,
they sang their hymns of praise;
to thee, now high exalted,
our melody we raise.
Thou didst accept their praises;
accept the prayers we bring,
who in all good delightest,
thou good and gracious King.

MH 46 All Glory, Laud, and Honor....SDAH 230
Theophilus of Orleans (750-821)
Tr. By John M. Neale (1818-1866)
Ekpeye Translation

1
Gbele gbele igili lo odhu esor,
Bu ayo Eze Udorkpewe
Nye mu ogbo umeledhe,
Gwu nyigbe orbu te etor,
Yo, Eze emene Isreal,
Yo, unwor Eze David,
Yo, nye mu ejor lewa Nye nweye
Eze li nyi uwokwani

2
Emene ogbo uzhi uma padhiwe gbe Yo lo olu,
Madu egedhe li gbele gbele iye,
Kpu gbe asaagbe Yo,
Emene Hebrews moji ormu kaze gbe lununu Yo,
Ya padhi li edhor li orbu Ya gala lununu Yo.

3
Muba dhuma eye akwu kwu,
Orgwu gbe orbu upadi
Ndekpu ububuze olu Yo zhile,
Lor orbu etor ye agwunyi Yo,
Yo ye natu upadhi gbe, natu upadhiwe ye,
Yo nye gbele gbele iye uma,
Eze uma li Ortizi

MH 47 Jesus, the Very Thought of Thee SDAH 241

Attrib. to Bernard of Clairvaux (1091-1153)
Tr. By Edward Caswell (1814-1878)

English

1
Jesus, the very thought of thee
with sweetness fills the breast;
but sweeter far thy face to see,
and in thy presence rest.

2
No voice can sing, no heart can frame,
Nor can the memory find
A sweeter sound than Jesus' name,
The Savior of mankind.

3
O hope of every contrite heart!
O joy of all the meek,
to those who fall, how kind thou art!
How good to those who seek!

4
But what to those who find? Ah, this
nor tongue nor pen can show;
the love of Jesus, what it is,
none but his loved ones know.

5
Jesus, our only joy be thou,
as thou our prize wilt be;
Jesus, be thou our glory now,
and through eternity.

MH 47 Jesus, the Very Thought of Thee SDAH 241
Attrib. to Bernard of Clairvaux (1091-1153)
Tr. By Edward Caswell (1814-1878)
Ekpeye Translation

1
Jesus egedhe ugbeweji Yo
Uyuluka obu me le etor
Uweji upi Yo kashi kpome
Lude eli li ime yo.

2
Unu kadhor ekpema medhor
Ugbedhiga wuweji dhor,
Iye iye torka ewa Jesus,
Nyu mu dorkpewe madu.

3
Unye unye ekpema nyu umeyeshi
Obu etor nyu uyodhu,
Nde usheka Yo le emene dagbe?
Nde iye uma emene wudhiga?

4
Ndekpu emene weji etor zhile?
Idho lu ukpalahu kadhor,
Iye ugwushi Jesus ubu,
Eemene ugwusha majigbe.

5
Jesus neten, ibu obu etor ye
Kpormu ibor iye gbu aya ye,
Lime Yo gbele, gbele esor ye zhi,
Ddhuma uwa ogbo ogbo.

MH 48 The Great Physician Now is Near SDAH 254

William Hunter, 1859 (1811-1877)

English

1

The great Physician now is near,
The sympathizing Jesus;
He speaks the drooping heart to cheer,
Oh! hear the voice of Jesus.

Chorus
Sweetest note in seraph song,
Sweetest name on mortal tongue;
Sweetest carol ever sung,
Jesus, blessed Jesus.

2

Your many sins are all forgiven,
Oh! hear the voice of Jesus;
Go on your way in peace to heaven,
And wear a crown with Jesus.

3

All glory to the dying Lamb!
I now believe in Jesus;
I love the blessed Savior's name,
I love the name of Jesus.

4

His name dispels my guilt and fear,
No other name but Jesus;
Oh! how my soul delights to hear
The charming name of Jesus.

MH 48 The Great Physician Now is Near SDAH 254

William Hunter, 1859 (1811-1877)

Ekpeye Translation

1
Nye eke dibia uzhilu uzedhu,
Nye eke ortizhi mu Jesus,
Ekpor Ya me nya agbezhi padhi
Nuji ekpor mu Jesus.

Chorus
Ekpor te etor, lor obu emene uzhi uma
Ewa te etor, li idhor madu
Orbu kakpo, orbu emene, orbu gwugbe,
Jesus uwokwani Jesus.

2
Gbele gbele esor, zhini ugaga nwulu
Me whetu lem li Jesus,
Mor gwushi ewa nyu dorkpewe me
Mor gwushi ewa Jesus.

3
Ewa, chimame idakpe li otogu,
Udor ewa zhe gama Jesus,
Kpu uwa me wudhigalu unuji,
Ewa, umamu Jesus.

4
Eke, ejor, lugala okpulushi Eze,
Okpulushi budu li odhu esor,
Ye anazhi ezhi lu ukwu eli Ya
lu udhor kala uka udorkpewe.

MH 49   Spirit Divine   SDAH 267
Andrew Reed, 1829 (1787-1862)
English

1
Spirit divine, attend our prayer,
And make this house Thy home;
Descend with all Thy gracious power;
Come, great Spirit, come!

2
Come as the light; to us reveal
Our emptiness and woe,
And lead us in those paths of light,
Whereon the righteous go.

3
Come as the fire and purge our hearts
Like sacrificial flame,
Let our whole soul an off'ring be
To our Redeemer's name.

4
Come as the dove and spread Thy wings,
The wings of peaceful love;
And let Thy church on earth become
Blest as the church above.

5
Spirit divine, attend our prayers,

Make a lost world Thy home;

Descend with all Thy gracious powers,

O come, great Spirit, come!

MH 49   Spirit Divine   SDAH 267

Andrew Reed, 1829 (1787-1862)

Ekpeye Translation

1
Uwuma Eblikpabi, jakejiye le edhor ye,
Mu igonu udhormu mime wetu ayo,
Kaja li gbele gbele ugbakpo Yo,
Kaja, Ekai uwuma ja.

2
Ja kpormu usamali,
Mu ilorwe eli yo,
Eka ewe ye, li iwene,
Mcc idu ye li ichakpa budu,
Li igbu emene uma zhedhe.

3
Ja kpormu echi, mu igwor ekpema ye,
Kpormu echi eja, me gbele gbele uwa ye,
iye orsorja Yo
Lewa nyu ugawe ye.

4
Ja kpormu gbili, mu igbati eyi Yo,
Eyi ugwushi uyodu mu church Yo,
Le eluwa zhi uwokwani,
Kpormi church zhi lolu.

5
Uwuma Eblikpabi jakejiye li edhor ye,
Mai mu uwam tadhom bu udhor Yo,
Jali gbele gbele ugbakpo,
Kaja ekai uwa ja.

MH 50   Only Trust Him   SDAH 279

J. H. Stockton (1813-1877)

English

1
Come, every soul by sin oppressed,
There's mercy with the Lord,
And He will surely give you rest,
By trusting in His word.

Chorus
Only trust Him, only trust Him,
Only trust Him now;
He will save you, He will save you,
He will save you now.

2
For Jesus shed his precious blood
Rich blessings to bestow;
Plunge now into the crimson flood
That washes white as snow.

3
Yes, Jesus is the truth, the way,
That leads you into rest;
Believe in Him without delay,
And you are fully blest.

4
Come, then, and join this holy band,
And on to glory go,
To dwell in that celestial land,
Where joys immortal flow.

MH 50   Only Trust Him   SDAH 279

J. H. Stockton (1813-1877)

Ekpeye Translation

1
Ja gbele gbele uwa umeyeshi jigbo,
Nye nwe ye bu nye ortizhi,
Le egedhe enedhe yo udeli
Lawu igbele obu yo lu uka Ya

Chorus
Ne-whuta obu yo, ne-whuta obu yo,
Ne-whuta obu yo lu umorm,
ordorkpewe yo, ordorkpewe yo,
ordorkpewe yo lu umorm.

2
Jesus wosa ubala uma mu aya,
Lu unedhe eke uwokwani,
Kpudhu lime ukputu ubala yo
Amu usamor kpormu mini orkpor eligwe.
3
Jesus bu ishishiuka la ichakpa,
Amu odushorYo lime uyodhu,
Whetu nya etashe ekele
Owokwani kpole yo.
4
Ja-keji ye mi zhi, logbo egwelem,
Mi ikaze lime odhu esor, mi ibe ele,
Ogbo emene uzhi uma,
Adhi obu etor lu ugwu unwulu ornwulu uzhi.

MH 51   Wonderful Words of Life   SDAH 286

P. P. Bliss (1874 (1838-1876)

English

1
Sing them over again to me,
wonderful words of life,
Let me more of their beauty see,
wonderful words of life;
Words of life and beauty
teach me faith and duty.

Chorus
Beautiful words, wonderful words,
wonderful words of life,
Beautiful words, wonderful words,
wonderful words of life.

2
Christ, the blessèd One, gives to all
wonderful words of life;
Sinner, list to the loving call,
wonderful words of life;
All so freely given,
wooing us to heaven.
3
Sweetly echo the Gospel call,
wonderful words of life;
Offer pardon and peace to all,
wonderful words of life;
Jesus, only Savior,
sanctify forever.

MH 51   Wonderful Words of Life   SDAH 286

P. P. Bliss (1874 (1838-1876)

Ekpeye Translation

1
Gwunyi gbam orbu udor
Ekpor unyodhawe enye budu
Mu nweji kpogba kpu ezor ya zhile
Ekpor unyodhawe enye budu
Ekpor budu li ezor
Zhimu uwhetu li ugbolo.

Chorus
Ekpor zorzor ekpor unyodha enye
Ekpor Unyodha enye budu
Ekpor zorzor ekpor ungodha enye
Ekpor unyodha enye budu

2
Christ, nyu uwokwani, nedhe ogbo,
Ekpor unyodha enye budu,
Nyu umeyeshi zeh uli uwhu ugwushi
Ekpor unyodhawe enye budu
Gbele gbele mu unedhi ewe,
Uwhue la gbe ye orbioma.

3
Le etor, chi ikpu uwhu uzhi uma,
Ekpor unyodha we enye budu,
Neh gbele gbele madu ortizhi li uyodhu
Ekpor unyodhawe enye budu
Jesus neten bu nyu ugawe
Umesama ya ugbo ogbo

MH 52   Softly and Tenderly   SDAH 287

Will L. Thompson (1847-1909)

English

1
Softly and tenderly Jesus is calling,
calling for you and for me;
see, on the portals he's waiting and watching,
watching for you and for me.

Chorus
Come home, come home;
ye who are weary come home;
earnestly, tenderly, Jesus is calling,
calling, O sinner, come home!

2
Why should we tarry when Jesus is pleading,
pleading for you and for me?
Why should we linger and heed not his mercies,
mercies for you and for me?

3
Think of the wonderful love he has promised,
promised for you and for me!
Though we have sinned, he has mercy and pardon,
pardon for you and for me.

MH 52   Softly and Tenderly   SDAH 287
Will L. Thompson (1847-1909)
Ekpeye Translation

1
Li uli ele, lor ortizhi, Jesus udhu uwhu,
Udhu uwhu yo li me,
Lu unobudhor ekpema Udhu seji udhu nyiji,
Unyiji yo li me

Chorus
Ya udhor, ya udhor
Yo nye eyi kali, ya udhor
Le egedhe, li ortizhi Jesus Udhu uwhu,
udhu uwhu nyu umeyeshi, ya udhor.

2
Nde iye aseji eke Jesus udhu udhor?
Udhu udhor yo li me,
Iyelador ma ashishiga ma awhie ortizhi ya?
Ortizhi yo li me.

3
Gbeji ugwushi unyodha enye ugwunyi ye egba
Ugwunyi yo li me,
Ye ameyele, unwe ortizhi li usabeteni
Usabeteni yo li me.

MH 53   Rock of Ages   SDAH 300
Augustus M. Toplady, 1776 (1740-1778)
English

1
Rock of Ages, cleft for me,
Let me hide myself in Thee;
Let the water and the blood,
From Thy riven side which flowed,
Be of sin the double cure,
Cleanse me from its guilt and power.
2
Not the labor of my hands
Can fulfill Thy law's demands;
Could my zeal no respite know,
Could my tears forever flow,
All for sin could not atone;
Thou must save, and Thou alone
3
When my pilgrimage I close;
Victor o'er the last of foes,
When I soar to worlds unknown,
And behold Thee on Thy throne,
Rock of Ages, cleft for me,
Let me hide myself in Thee.

MH 53   Rock of Ages   SDAH 300
Augustus M. Toplady, 1776 (1740-1778)
Ekpeye Translation

1
Igwu ukani, ugbagala me,
Woke mu li ime yo,
Mini li ubala, gba malior
li ukwu yo, bu iye gwor kakpor umeye,
samam li idakpe li, ugbakpo ya.

2
Uborle eka ugbolo me,
Ozukpo oloko ma aada
Ekeh ugbakpo me amaje udeli,
Ishigili ikwame ndeke ogbo ogbo,
Iye obugama ogbo umeye-shim zhe,
Yo neten, egawe ye.

3
Eke mezekpo uzhi me
Lugbo nyegba gwulu orgwulu,
Eke makaze eluwa maa majem,
Weji yo la agida Eze Yo,
Igwu ukani ugbagala me,
Woke mu li ime Yo.

MH 54   Faith of Our Fathers   SDAH 304

Frederick W. Faber, 1849 (1814-1863)

English

1
Faith of our fathers, living still,
In spite of dungeon, fire and sword;
O how our hearts beat high with joy
Whenever we hear that glorious Word!
Faith of our fathers, holy faith!
We will be true to thee till death.

2
Our fathers, chained in prisons dark,
Were still in heart and conscience free:
How sweet would be their children's fate.
If they, like them, could die for thee!
Faith of our fathers, holy faith!
We will be true to thee till death.

3
Faith of our fathers, we will love
Both friend and foe in all our strife;
And preach Thee, too, as love knows how
By kindly words and virtuous life.
Faith of our fathers, holy faith!
We will be true to thee till death.

MH 54   Faith of Our Fathers   SDAH 304
Frederick W. Faber, 1849 (1814-1863)
Ekpeye Translation

1
Uwhetu emene eda ye zhi budu,
Utunye gbe enwu, li echi, li oge
Ndekpu obu etor ye uzhile
Leke anujile uka uma Ya,
Uwhetu emene eda ye zhi egwele
Ye ya zhi nyor yo li
Ishishuka dhuma cnwu.

2
Uchegbe emene eda ye
Iyagba li ikoli unazhi gbe lunukwuma usa
Ndekpu etor uwhutu umeledhe zhile
Bule kporm gbe nwulorgbe lishi yo,
Uwhetu emene eda ye, zhi ya zhi egwele,
Ye ya zhi nyor yo li ishishuka dhuma enwu.

3
Uwhetu emene eda ye ye agwushi,
Nwuje li nye egba li ime orwele,
lu zhikala kpu ugwushi Yo zhile,
Le ekpor uyodhu li agwa uma,
Uwhetu emene eda ye zhi egwele, ye ya zhi
nyor yo li ishishuka dhuma enwu.

MH 55   Draw Me Nearer   SDAH 306

Fanny J. Crosby, 1875 (1820-1915)

English

1
I am thine, O Lord, I have heard thy voice,
and it told thy love to me;
but I long to rise in the arms of faith
and be closer drawn to thee.

Chorus
Draw me nearer, nearer, blessed Lord,
to the cross where thou hast died.
Draw me nearer, nearer, nearer, blessed Lord,
to thy precious, bleeding side.

2
Consecrate me now to thy service, Lord,
by the power of grace divine;
let my soul look up with a steadfast hope,
and my will be lost in thine.

3
O the pure delight of a single hour
that before thy throne I spend,
when I kneel in prayer, and with thee, my God,
I commune as friend with friend!

MH 55   Draw Me Nearer   SDAH 306

Fanny J. Crosby, 1875 (1820-1915)

Ekpeye Translation

1
Morbu ayo, Eblikpabi, mornujilem uli yo,
Amu ukor ugwushi inwe li elime,
Medhu zhi lu uwudhiga, luzhi le, eka uwhetu,
Mu umanu nzhi uzegbu le yo.

Chorus
Doryamu ukwu,Ukwu Eda zhi uwokwani
Lu ushi uye lu uka mu enwulor,
Doryamu ukwu ukwu Eda zhi uwokwani
Li ibe mu ubala yo gbalorshor

2
Eda,gbemu le egwele,
Lu unazhi lu ugbolo yo,
Lu ugbakpo ortizhi Eblikpabi,
Mu uwa me, nye lo olu, lu unuzo, lu uwhetu,
Mu umanu udorshime lu ukwu yo

3
Umawunu unazhi, lu unu ugbe ntuko ,
Lu ununu agida eze mu ayo,
Eke mejile ukpunuko , lu ukpeni Yo,
Eblikpabi akadhi kpormu nwuje li nwuje,

MH 56   I Surrender All   SDAH 309

J. W. VanDeVenter, 1896 (1855-1939)

English

1
All to Jesus I surrender;
all to him I freely give;
I will ever love and trust him,
in his presence daily live.

Chorus
I surrender all, I surrender all,
all to thee, my blessed Savior,
I surrender all.

2
All to Jesus I surrender;
humbly at his feet I bow,
worldly pleasures all forsaken;
take me, Jesus, take me now.

3
All to Jesus I surrender;
make me, Savior, wholly thine;
fill me with thy love and power;
truly know that thou art mine.

4
All to Jesus I surrender;
now I feel the sacred flame.
O the joy of full salvation!
Glory, glory, to his name!

MH 56   I Surrender All   SDAH 309
J. W. VanDeVenter, 1896 (1855-1939)
Ekpeye Translation

1
Gbele gbele mu menekpo Jesus
Gbele gbele mu menekpo lema,
Mor gwusha me shishi obu me
Li ime ya gbele gbele eye.

Chorus
Menekpolema, Menekpolema,
Menekpolema, Menekpolema,
Mene Yo, Nyu uwokwani ugawe me,
Menekpolemi

2
Gbele gbele mu, menekpo Jesus,
Lu uko ya ma-gbadawe ishi,
Etor uwa ma sabete kpolemu
Gonumu Jesus, gonumu lu umorm.

3
Gbele gbele mu menekpo Jesus,
 Mewemu, Nye new me ayo,
Mweji uwa egwele mu ayo,
Mu maji gbibu ame legedhe

4
Gbele gbele me nekpo Jesus,
Echi uyodhu zhili ime me,
Le ekpema etor ordorkpewe e me
Esor, esor, zhini ewa ya.

MH 57   Power in the Blood   SDAH 294

Lewis E. Jones, 1899 (1865-1936)

English

1

Would you be free from the burden of sin?
There's pow'r in the blood,pow'r in the blood;
Would you o'er evila victory win?
There's wonderful power in the blood.

Chorus

There is pow'r, pow'r, wonder working pow'r
In the blood of the Lamb;
There is pow'r, pow'r, wonder working pow'r
In the precious blood of the Lamb.

2

Would be free from your passion and pride?
There's pow'r in the blood, pow'r in the blood;
Come for a cleansing to Calvary's tide?
There's wonderful power in the blood.

3

Would you do service for Jesus your King?
There's pow'r in the blood, pow'r in the blood;
Would you live daily His praises to sing?
There's wonderful power in the blood.

MH 57   Power in the Blood   SDAH 294

Lewis E. Jones, 1899 (1865-1936)

Ekpeye Translation

1
Ye egbamalile lu'ubuu umeyeshi?
Ugbakpo zhi lime ubala, ugbakpo zhi lime ubula,
Ye emegbokpole ogbo iyegbiyor?
Ugakpo unwodha enye zhi lime ubala.

Chorus
Ugbakpo zhi, zhi, ume ugbolo unwodha enye
Lu ubala, ugaga
Ugbakpo zhi, zhi, ume ugbolo unwodha enye
Lu ubala ugaga mu ugbuayam.

2
Ye egbamalile lime akwakwu li ide yo?
Ugbakpo zhi lime ubala, ugbakpo zhi lime ubala,
Jaa miba samayo li mini calvary,
Ugbakpo unwodha enye zhili ime ubala.

3
Emeni Jesus eze yo ugbolo?
Ugbakpo zhi lime ubala, ugbakpo zhi lime ubala.
Ebe bube mu epadhiwa gbele gbele eyeh
Ugbakpo unwodha enye zhi lime ubala.

MH 58   Near the Cross   SDAH 312

James Rowe (1865-1933)

English

1
Jesus, keep me near the cross;
there a precious fountain,
free to all, a healing stream,
flows from Calvary's mountain.

Chorus
In the cross, in the cross,
be my glory ever,
till my raptured soul shall find
rest beyond the river.

2
Near the cross, a trembling soul,
love and mercy found me;
there the bright and morning star
sheds its beams around me.

3
Near the cross! O Lamb of God,
bring its scenes before me;
help me walk from day to day
with its shadow o'er me.

4
Near the cross I'll watch and wait,
hoping, trusting ever,
till I reach the golden strand
just beyond the river.

MH 58   Near the Cross   SDAH 312

James Rowe (1865-1933)

English
Ekpeye Translation
1
Jesus, gbem lu ukwu ushi uye li uka,
Adhi mu mini uma gbor,
Adhi ogbo mini ugwor eli,
Gbalorshio le egbu calvary.

Chorus
Lu ushi uye li uka
Lu ushi uye li uka,
Bu esor me orgwulu, orgwulu,
Dhuma eke uma me eweji, udeli lorzu olimini.

2
Ukwu ushi uye li uka uwa hudhi
Ugwushi li ortizhi weji me
Adhi orkpudhor egbuluka oyukwe,
Lorwe nwudhi ya lu ushikoshi me.

3
Lukwu ushiuye li uka ugaga,
Eblikpabi, lorwe muladhi iyeya,
Memu nkaze gbele gbele eye
Ya le enyeh ya lolu me.

4
Ukwu ushi uye li uka me nyiji me seji,
Uwhetu ushushi obu, gbele gbele ekele
Dhuma eke nnuzo le, ekpe ekpuligwu ezor
Lu ugama oli-mini.

MH 59   Just as I Am   SDAH 313

Charlotte Elliot, 1834 (1789-1871)

English

1
Just as I am, without one plea,
But that Thy blood was shed for me,
And that Thou bidst me come to Thee,
O Lamb of God, I come, I come.

2
Just as I am, and waiting not
To rid my soul of one dark blot,
To Thee whose blood can cleanse each spot,
O Lamb of God, I come, I come.

3
Just as I am, though tossed about
With many a conflict, many a doubt,
"Fightings within, and fears without,"
O Lamb of God, I come, I come.

4
Just as I am, poor, wretched, blind;
Sight, riches, healing of the mind,
Yea, all I need in Thee to find,
O Lamb of God, I come, I come.

5
Just as I am, Thou wilt receive,
Wilt welcome, pardon, cleanse, relieve;
Because Thy promise I believe,
O Lamb of God, I come, I come.

MH 59   Just as I Am   SDAH 313
Charlotte Elliot, 1834 (1789-1871)
Ekpeye Translation

1
Le kporm mezhom iye edhor zhe
Ubala yo wosali li me,
Uubu Yo ihume meja
Ugaga Ebilkpabi mmume.

2
Le kporm mezhom, lu ugu useji
Lu unama unye lime uwa me,
Yo nyu ubala Ya asama unye ya,
Ugaga Eblikpabi, mmume.

3
Le kporm mezhom, unukoshi gbeme adhi,
Lo ogbo orwele li ogbo unwodha enye,
Lime ulu li ugutu otogu
Ugaga Eblikpabi, mumme

4
Le kporm mezhom, ogboyi, uyaa, enyekpor
Uweji ahdi le ekpe lu ugwor ekpema me,
Iye korshi me, mo wuwejilo yo
Ugaga eblikpabi mmume.

5
Le kporm mezhom ye, enatu
Usabeteni usama, ubugamani;
Iyedor mewhetu le egba yo,
Ugaga eblikpabi mmume.

6
Le kporm mezhom ugwushi yo me new
Iye tashim iye ordorkakpole;
Lu umorm lu ubu ayo neten;
Ugaga Eblikpabi mmume.

MH 60   My Jesus, I Love Thee   SDAH 321
William Ralf Featherstone (1846-1873)
English

1

My Jesus, I love thee, I know thou art mine;
for thee all the follies of sin I resign.
My gracious Redeemer, my Savior art thou;
if ever I loved thee, my Jesus, 'tis now.

2

I love thee because thou hast first loved me,
and purchased my pardon on Calvary's tree;
I love thee for wearing the thorns on thy brow;
if ever I loved thee, my Jesus, 'tis now.

3

I'll love Thee in life, I will love Thee 'til death,
And praise Thee as long as Thou lendest me breath;
And say when the death dew lies cold on my brow,
if ever I loved thee, my Jesus, 'tis now.

4

In mansions of glory and endless delight;
I'll ever adore thee in heaven so bright;
I'll sing with the glittering crown on my brow;
if ever I loved thee, my Jesus, 'tis now.

MH 60   My Jesus, I Love Thee   SDAH 321
William Ralf Featherstone (1846-1873)
Ekpeye Translation

1
Jesus, mor gwushiYo, ma maji ibu ame
Lishi Yo gbele gbele, umeyeshi me morlor, kpolema
Ibu egedhe nyu udorkpewe me li egedhe nyu ugawe
Bule gbumor gwushi yo, Jesus, ubulu umorm.

2
Mor gwushi yo iyedor igwushi me lu unuzu
Igo usabetenyi me lu ushi Calvary,
Mor gwushi yo lu ukpuji okpulishi ngu lishi me
Bule gbumor gwushu yo Jesus, ubu lu umorm.

3
Mor gwushi yo li budu, mor gwushi yo dhuma enwu,
Maa apadhiwe Yo kpu budu ineme uzhile
Maa ka leke Igiligi li ukagi enwu da lishi me;
Bule gbu mor gwushi Yo, Jesus ubu lu umorm.

4
Lime eke udhor igili lu umashi ogbo ogbo
Mai kpeni dhidhi yo li orbioma zorzor,
Morgwu orbu okpulizhi eze mu dhu unwudhior lishi me,
Bule gbu mor gwushi yo jesus ubu lu umorm.

MH 61   Take My Life and Let It Be SDAH 330
Frances Ridley Havergal, 1874 (1836-1879)
English

1
Take my life, and let it be
Consecrated, Lord, to Thee;
Take my hands, and let them move
At the impulse of Thy love;
At the impulse of Thy love.
2
Take my feet, and let them be
Swift and beautiful for Thee.
Take my voice, and let me sing
Always, only, for my King;
Always, only, for my King.
3
Take my lips, and let them be
Filled with messages from Thee.
Take my silver and my gold:
Not a mite would I withhold;
Not a mite would I withhold.
4
Take my will, and make it Thine,
It shall be no longer mine;
Take my heart, it is Thine own,
It shall be Thy royal throne.
It shall be Thy royal throne.

5
Take my love, my Lord, I pour
At Thy feet its treasure store;
Take myself, and I will be,
Ever, only, all for Thee.
Ever, only, all for Thee.

MH 61   Take My Life and Let It Be SDAH 330
Frances Ridley Havergal, 1874 (1836-1879)
Ekpeye Translation

1
Gonu budu memeke uzhi
Egwele, Nye nwe ye, le ewa Yo
Gonu eka me mu ugadhiga
Li unu ugwushi mu ayo
Li unu ugwushi mu ayo

2
Gonu uko me meke uzhi gbe
Ezor lu ukporni yo enwa
Gonu uli me mu nguni Yo orbu,
Mu nguni eze me gbele gbele ekele.
Mu nguni eze me gbele gbele ekele
3
Gonu ugbanu me meke uzhigbe
Mu uzegbe uzhi buzeli le eka yo
Gonu silver me li gold me
Nna mamu iye iye lime ya.
Nna mamu iye iye lime ya.
4
Gonu echiche me mime wetu ayo;
Ndeke orbor dhe ame,
Gonu ekpema ubutu ayo,
Orbuhor agida eze yo.
Orbuhor agida eze yo
5
Gonu ugwushi me, nye Nwe ye me ne
Lu uko yo udhor ugbckc ckpe;
Gonu me meke morbu;
Li gbele gbele iye me zhini ohor yo.

MH 62　　　Jesus Saves　　　SDAH 340
Priscilla J. Owens (1829-1907)
English

1
We have heard a joyful sound,
Jesus saves, Jesus saves;
Spread the gladness all around,
Jesus saves, Jesus saves;
Bear the news to every land,
Climb the steeps and cross the waves,
Onward 'tis our Lord's command,
Jesus saves, Jesus saves.

2
Waft it on the rolling tide,
Jesus saves, Jesus saves;
Tell to sinners, far and wide,
Jesus saves, Jesus saves;
Sing, ye islands of the sea,
Echo back, ye ocean caves,
Earth shall keep her jubilee,
Jesus saves, Jesus saves.

3
Sing above the battle's strife,
Jesus saves, Jesus saves;
By His death and endless life,
Jesus saves, Jesus saves;
Sing it softly through the gloom,
When the heart for mercy craves,
Sing in triumph o'er the tomb,
Jesus saves, Jesus saves.

MH 62   Jesus Saves   SDAH 340
Priscilla J. Owens (1829-1907)
Ekpeye Translation

1
Anuji uka ekpema etor,
Jesus gawe, Jesus gawe;
Memu obu etor ya zuke,
Jesus gawe Jesus gawe;
Zhikala li gbele gbele adhi,
Kpegbu, lo olu, wekpe uwoshi,
Umeze bu iye nye new ye ka,
Jesus gawe, Jesus gawe.

2
Gawaa li ugbadhe orwayi
Jesus gawe, Jesus gawe;
Kani nyu umeyeshi gbele gbele adhi,
Jesus gawe, Jesus gawe;
Umu ele zhi le eke mini adhi
Chilawe ikpu yo eke mini;
Eluwa egbele eye upadhi,
Jesus gawe Jesus gawe.

3
Gwunyi orbu emene ulu,
Jesus gawe. Jesus gawe
Le enwu ya li budu ogbo ogbo,
Jesus gawe, Jesus gawe;
Gwua luli eli eli leke agbezhi,
Leke ekpema wudhiga ortizhi,
Gwu orbu utu ugo le olu ili,
Jesus gawe Jesus gawe.

MH 62   Jesus Saves   SDAH 340
Priscilla J. Owens (1829-1907)
English

4
Give the winds a mighty voice,
Jesus saves, Jesus saves;
Let the nations now rejoice,
Jesus saves, Jesus saves;
Shout salvation full and free,
Highest hills and deepest caves,
This our song of victory,
Jesus saves, Jesus saves.

MH 62   Jesus Saves   SDAH 340
Priscilla J. Owens (1829-1907)
Ekpeye Translation

4
Nedhe uwele uli ube eke,
Jesus gawe, Jesus gawe,
Ula torhorni ekpema,
Jesus gawe, Jesus gawe,
Chi gbu ugawe bu iye unedhi,
Ewe eke egbu li eke ugbu,
Orbu umegbo bu aye,
Jesus gawe Jesus gawe.

MH 63   I Will Sing of My Redeemer SDAH 343

Philip P. Bliss, 1876 (1838-1876)

English

1
I will sing of my Redeemer,
And His wondrous love to me;
On the cruel cross He suffered,
From the curse to set me free.

Chorus
Sing, oh sing, of my Redeemer,
With His blood, He purchased me.
On the cross, He sealed my pardon,
Paid the debt, and made me free.

2
I will tell the wondrous story,
How my lost estate to save,
In His boundless love and mercy,
He the ransom freely gave.

3
I will sing of my Redeemer,
And His heavenly love to me;
He from death to life hath brought me,
Son of God with Him to be.

MH 63   I Will Sing of My Redeemer SDAH 343

Philip P. Bliss, 1876 (1838-1876)

Ekpeye Translation

1
Maa gbabuze ewa, Nyu ugawe me,
Lu uguwushi unwodha enye, unwe li me,
Le olu ushi uye lu uka tanyi me akwukwu
Lu udorkpeme la umekpeli.

Chorus
Gwu, gwuni iye kpani nyu ugawe me,
Lu ubala ya ugawe me,
Lu ushi uye li uka uwhetu usabeteni,
Uwhudhi ugor udorkpewe me

2
Mordhor kala uka unwodha enye,
Kpu ekpe me wulu li kpu ulorle
Le eke ugwushi lor ortizhi ma Ya,
Iye ugowe me uneme ewe.

3
Maa gbauze ewa Nyu gawe me
Lu ugwushi orbioma ya le me,
Udorkpewe me lime ewhu
Mu nzhi-keji unwor Eblikpabi.

MH 64   Give Me the Bible   SDAH 272

Priscilla J. Owens (1829-1907)

English

1
Give me the Bible, star of gladness gleaming,
To cheer the wanderer lone and tempest tossed,
No storm can hide that peaceful radiance beaming
Since Jesus came to seek and save the lost.

Chorus
Give me the Bible-holy message shining,
Thy light shall guide me in the narrow way.
Precept and promise, law and love combining,
'Til night shall vanish in eternal day.

2
Give me the Bible when my heart is broken,
When sin and grief have filled my soul with fear,
Give me the precious words by Jesus spoken,
Hold up faith's lamp to show my Savior near.

3
Give me the Bible, all my steps enlighten,
Teach me the danger of these realms below,
That lamp of safety, o'er the gloom shall brighten,
That light alone the path of peace can show.

MH 64   Give Me the Bible   SDAH 272

Priscilla J. Owens (1829-1907)

Ekpeye Translation

1
Nemu ukpalahu egwele,
Okpudhor egbuluka obu etor,
Lu upadhiwe nyo nwulu lime eke uwele
Uzhe eke uwele owoke dho obu etor uzhikpe,
Jesus ja mu udor emen wulugbe.

Chorus
Nemu ukpalahu egwele , uzhi egwele nwulorshi
Echi yo odume le ichakpo ntukor,
Umeke iye li ugwu egba, oloka lu ugwushi megbedhe legbe
Dhuma eke abali dhili lime eye

2
Nemu ukpalahu egwele leke ekpema tadhule
Leke agbezhi li umeyeshi ne uwa me otogu,
Nemu uli ekpor uma Jesus kanidhe ye,
Mojike echi uwhetu lorwe Nye gawe uzedhu.

3
Nemu ukpalabu egwele, gbele gbele usamali edanduko me,
zhimu iye otogu lu ukpudhu ele ezem ayo
Tonjor ugawe, echima igeleni usamali ya neten,
Ichakpa uyodhu orlor.

MH 65   I Heard the Voice of Jesus SDAH 465

Horatius Bonar (1808-1889)

English

1

I heard the voice of Jesus say,
"Come unto Me and rest;
Lay down, thou weary one, lay down
Thy head upon My breast."
I came to Jesus as I was,
Weary and worn and sad;
I found in Him a resting place,
And He has made me glad.

2

I heard the voice of Jesus say,
"Behold, I freely give
The living water; thirsty one,
Stoop down and drink and live."
I came to Jesus, and I drank
Of that life giving stream;
My thirst was quench'd, my soul revived,
And now I live in Him.

3

I heard the voice of Jesus say,
"I am this dark world's light;
Look unto Me, thy morn shall rise,
And all thy day be bright."
I looked to Jesus, and I found
In Him my star, my sun;
And in that light of life I'll walk,
Till trav'ling days are done

MH 65   I Heard the Voice of Jesus SDAH 465

Horatius Bonar (1808-1889)
Ekpeye Translation

1
Mornuji uli Jesus ka,
Jakejim mideyo eli,
Dagbete nye elida dagbete,
Ishi yo leli me,
Mejakeji Jesus kpume zhile,
Eli uda lu uwudhu uma,
Meweja kpormu adhi udeli,
Une me ekpema etor

2
Mornuji, uli Jesus ka,
Notu, mene-dhi ewe,
Mini budu nye ekidhi kpe,
Tukpu menwu me izhi
Meja keji Jesus mumornwo,
Mini mu, nedhor budum
Ugwulu ekidhi ukpeme ne
Uyodhu, lu umorm mebe lime ya.

3
Mornuji, uli Jesus ka,
Morbu usamali igeleni uwa
Weji-me, mo owukwe yo borli,
Me eye yo nwumali,
Okpudhor egbuluka li elanwu me,
Ma kaze lu usamali budu
Dhuma eke izeya gwulu

MH 66   I'd Rather Have Jesus   SDAH 327

Rhea F. Miller, 1922 (1894-1966)

English

1
I'd rather have Jesus than silver or gold;
I'd rather be His than have riches untold;
I'd rather have Jesus than houses or land;
I'd rather be led by His nail-pierced hand:

Chorus
*Than to be the king of a vast domain or be
held in sin's dread sway!
I'd rather have Jesus than anything this
world affords today.*

2
I'd rather have Jesus than men's applause;
I'd rather be faithful to His dear cause;
I'd rather have Jesus than world-wide fame;
I'd rather be true to His holy name:

3
He's fairer than lilies of rarest bloom;
He's sweeter than honey from out the comb;
He's all that my hungering spirit needs –
I'd rather have Jesus and let Him lead:

MH 66   I'd Rather Have Jesus   SDAH 327

Rhea F. Miller, 1922 (1894-1966)

Ekpeye Translation

Umanu me nwe Jesus, ka silver li gold,
Umanu morbu a-ya, ka unwe ekpetu ogbo,
Umanu me nwe Jesus, ka udhor le ele,
Umanu meke udu me leka enyigbom ma ya

Chorus
Ka ubu eze li ighu ube eke,
Lu ube ligili umeyeshi,
Umanu me nwe Jesus ka iye li iye bu,
Eluwa ene me tam

2
Umanu me nwe Jesus, ka utushi uwa,
Umanu me zhili uwhetu li iye kpani ya,
Umanu me nwe Jesus, ka eke ewa uwa,
Umanu me zhi lishushu-ka
Le ewa egwele ma ya

3
Orzor kale anwu ushi, kakpoligbe,
Ortor kale orga orgbeyi ulor uwu,
Ubu gbele gbele ugwunu, ugwu uwa me,
Umanu me nwe Jesus, meke udu me

MH 67   My Faith Looks Up to Thee   SDAH 517

Ray Palmer, 1830 (1808-1887)

English

1

My faith looks up to thee,
thou Lamb of Calvary,
Savior divine;
Now hear me while I pray,
take all my guilt away,
O let me from this day
be wholly Thine.

2

May thy rich grace impart
strength to my fainting heart,
my zeal inspire!
As thou hast died for me,
O may my love to thee
pure, warm, and changeless be,
a living fire!

3

While life's dark maze I tread,
and griefs around me spread,
be thou my guide;
bid darkness turn to day,
wipe sorrow's tears away,
nor let me ever stray
from Thee aside.

MH 67   My Faith Looks Up to Thee   SDAH 517

Ray Palmer, 1830 (1808-1887)

Ekpeye Translation

1
Uwhetu me nye li yo
Ugaga Calvary,
Nyu ugawe me,
Nuji edhor mor dhor,
Nama ida kpe me godhu li tam kaze,
Morbu hor ayo

2
Ortizhi aliye ma Ayo,
Nedhe ekpema me Ugbakpo,
Ume mu ugwo me kike,
Kpormu enwulu nye me,
Ugwushi me li yo
Umanor ugwe ugbanwo,
Echi budu.

3
Igeleni budu ma kaze,
Agbezhi shikoshi gbeme,
Bu nyu udu me,
Me mu igeleni be eye,
Kwo mam ishigili ekwa, agbezhi
Godhu li tam kaze,
Morbu hor Ayo

MH 68   Jerusalem, My Happy Home .....SDAH 420

Anon, c 1585

English

1
Jerusalem, my happy home,
O how I long for thee!
When will my sorrows have an end,
The joys when shall I see?

2
The walls are all of precious stone,
Most glorious to behold;
Thy gates are richly set with pearl,
Thy streets are paved with gold.

3
Thy garden and thy pleasant walks
My study long have been;
Such dazzling views by human sight
Have never yet been seen.

4
Lord, help us by Thy mighty grace,
To keep in view the prize,
Till Thou dost come to take us home
To that blessed paradise.

MH 68   Jerusalem, My Happy Home .....SDAH 420
Anon, c 1585
Ekpeye Translation

1
Jerusalem, udhor obu etor me
Ndekppu mehu nyele enye yo?
Ndeye agbezhi, orgwulu nime,
Ndeye meweji upadhi yo?

2
Ekwu udhor Yo, bu ekpuligwu Ugbu aya,
Iye kakpolighe lunwe,
Egbeleta yo umewagbe uchi zorzor,
Ichakpa yo utewagbe gold
3

Ika li okpe ika ezor mu Ayo,
Mormudhi gwulu lema
Adhi unyudhi kpe lenye umumadu,
Uka wejegbe lawuzu
4
Nye nwe ye, shishi nyiye eka
lu ugbeji adhi uma yo,
Dhuma eke ejor milawe ye udhor,
Ele eze uwokwani

MH 69   Sweet By and By SDAH 428

S. F. Bennett, 1867 (1836-1898)

English

1

There's a land that is fairer than day,
And by faith we can see it afar;
For the Father waits over the way
To prepare us a dwelling place there.

Chorus

In the sweet in the sweet
By and by by and by,
We shall meet on that beautiful shore;
In the sweet in the sweet
By and by by and by
We shall meet on that beautiful shore.

2

We shall sing on that beautiful shore
The melodious songs of the blest,
And our spirits shall sorrow no more
Not a sigh for the blessing of rest.
3

To our bountiful father above
We will offer our tribute of praise;
For the glorious gift of His love
And the blessings that hallow our days.

MH 69   Sweet By and By SDAH 428

S. F. Bennett, 1867 (1836-1898)

Ekpeye Translation

1
Uzhi ele uzorzor kaeye,
Lu uwhetu aweja takpu utor,
Eda ye esejike li ichakpa,
Mumeke nyiye adhi ubebe.

Chorus
Le etor ya, emekpor
Azuta le ele uma ya
Le etor ya, emekpor
Azuta le ele uma ya,

2
Agwor orbu etor le ule uma ya,
Orbu etor mu nyu uwokwani,
Uwa ye ndeke agbalezhi udhor,
Uta zhe lu uwokwani udeli
3
Ane Eda mu zhili orbioma upadhi,
lu une ye iye uma zhili ugwushi Ya
Agwu orbu upadhi le ewa ya
lu uwokwani mu uwokwa nyo ye.

MH 70 I'm But a Stranger Here   SDAH 445

Thomas R. Taylor, 1835 (1807-1835)

English

1
I'm but a stranger here,
Heav'n is my home;
Earth is a desert drear,
Heav'n is my home.
Danger and sorrow stand
Round me on every hand;
Heav'n is my fatherland,
Heav'n is my home.

2
What though the tempest rage,
Heav'n is my home;
Short is my pilgrimage,
Heav'n is my home;
And time's wild wintry blast
Soon shall be over past;
I shall reach home at last,
Heav'n is my home.

3
There at my Savior's side
Heav'n is my home;
I shall be glorified,
Heav'n is my home;
There are the good and blest,
Those I love most and best;
And there I, too, shall rest,
Heav'n is my home.

MH 70   I'm But a Stranger Here   SDAH 445

Thomas R. Taylor, 1835 (1807-1835)

Ekpeye Translation

1
Morbu nyize la adhim,
Orbioma bu udhor me,
Eluwa bu ele iwho,
Orbioma bu udhor me,
Otoggu li agbezhi,
Shikoshi me gbele gbele adhi,
Orbioma bu ele Eda me
Orbioma bu udhor me

2
Ubule kporm gbu eke uwele we,
Orbioma bu udhor me,
Ekele uzhi uma me zhi ntukor,
Orbioma bu udhor me,
Adhi lashee mo okidhika da,
Agashor bu enwe enwa,
Mo dhuma bu udhor me,
Orbioma bu udhor me.

3
Lu ukwu eli nyu gawe me,
Orbioma bu udhor me,
Ekenyor gbeme ekeni,
Orbioma bu udhor me,
Adhi emene uma li uwokwani,
Emene mor gwushi kakpoligbe,
Abu adhi udelii me,
Orbioma bu udhor me

MH 71   Leaning on the Everlasting Arms   SDAH 469
E. A. Hoffman, 1887 (1839-1929)
English

1
What a fellowship, what a joy divine,
leaning on the everlasting arms;
what a blessedness, what a peace is mine,
leaning on the everlasting arms.
Chorus
Leaning, leaning,
safe and secure from all alarms;
leaning, leaning,
leaning on the everlasting arms.
2
O how sweet to walk in this pilgrim way,
leaning on the everlasting arms;
O how bright the path grows from day to day,
leaning on the everlasting arms.
3
What have I to dread, what have I to fear,
leaning on the everlasting arms?
I have blessed peace with my Lord so near,
leaning on the everlasting arms.

MH 71   Leaning on the Everlasting Arms   SDAH 469

E. A. Hoffman, 1887 (1839-1929)
Ekpeye Translation

1
Ndekpu ukpa ya zhile, Ndekpu Obuetor ya zhile
Lu udabeni, le eka mu adada,
Ndekpu uwokwani ezhile
Ndepku uyodhu me ezhile
Lu udabeni, le eka mu adada;

Chorus
Lu udabeni, lu udabeni
Lu udorkpewe li gbele gbele iye otogu,
Lu udabeni, lu udabeni
Lu udabeni le eka mu adada

2
Ndekpu etor ukaze, Le ichakpa uzhi uma,
Lu udabeni le eka mu adada,
Ndekpu ezor okpe ya zhile le eye le eye,
Lu udabeni le eka adada

3
Ndiye mor sukornini, Ndiye mo tunyi ogwu,
Lu udabeni le eka mu adada
Me nwe uwokwani uyodhu, Lu uzedhu nye nwe ye,
Lu udabeni le ekamu adada.

MH 72   There's Sunshine in My Soul Today   SDAH 470

E. E. Hewitt (1851-1920)

English

1

There's sunshine in my soul today,
More glorious and bright
Than glows in any earthly sky,
For Jesus is my light.

Chorus
O there's sunshine, blessed sunshine,
When the peaceful, happy moments roll
When Jesus shows His smiling face
There is sunshine in the soul.

2

There's music in my soul today,
A carol to my King,
And Jesus, listening, can hear
The songs I cannot sing.

3

There's springtime in my soul today,
For when the Lord is near,
The dove of peace sings in my heart,
The flowers of grace appear.

4

There's gladness in my soul today,
And hope, and praise, and love,
For blessings which He gives me now,
For joys "laid up" above.

MH 72   There's Sunshine in My Soul Today   SDAH 470

E. E. Hewitt (1851-1920)

Ekpeye Translation

1
Usamali elanwu zhili uwa tam,
Eke utushi li unwumali,
Uka unwumali lolu eluwa,
Jesus bu usamali me

Chorus
Usamali elanwu, uwokwani usamali,
Leke uyodhu lı obuetor zhile,
Leke Jesus lorwele upi umu ma Ya,
Usamali elanwu uzhi lime uwa me.

2
Uli orbu zhi lu uwa me tam,
Orbu tor etor ugwunieze me,
Jesus kpete mu unuji,
Orbum mor orgwu dhomu

3
Uzhi uzordhu zhili uwa me tam,
Leke nye nwe ye zhili uzedhu
Gbilu uyodhu gworbe le ekpema me,
Anwu ushi uyodu mu lorgbe

4
Ekpema etor zhili uwa ma tam,
Unye enye upadhi li ugwushi,
Lu uwokwani mu neme lu umorm,
Lo obu etorm gbeni me lo olu

MH 73   Nearer My God, to Thee   SDAH 473

Sarah F. Adams, 1841 (1805-1848)

English

1
Nearer, my God, to thee, nearer to thee!
E'en though it be a cross that raiseth me,
still all my song shall be,
nearer, my God, to thee, nearer to thee!

2
Though like the wanderer, the sun gone down,
darkness be over me, my rest a stone;
yet in my dreams I'd be
nearer, my God, to thee, nearer to thee!

3
There let the way appear, steps unto heaven;
all that thou sendest me, in mercy given;
angels to beckon me
nearer, my God, to thee, nearer to thee!

4
Then, with my waking thoughts bright with thy praise,
out of my stony griefs Bethel I'll raise;
so by my woes to be
nearer, my God, to thee, nearer to thee!
5
Or if, on joyful wing cleaving the sky,
sun, moon, and stars forgot, upward I fly,
still all my song shall be,
nearer, my God, to thee, nearer to thee!

MH 73   Nearer My God, to Thee   SDAH 473

Sarah F. Adams, 1841 (1805-1848)

Ekpeye Translation

1
Eblikpabi zhi uzedhu, zhimu uzedhu,
Umashi gbu ushi oye li uka, gbabuze mo olu,
Gbele gbele orbu me ubu,
Eblikpabi zhi uzedhu, zhi mu uzedu

2
Kpormu nyu ukpeyega, uwechi agale,
Igeleni dashi me, udeli nwu uwe,
Li gbudhor me, morbu,
Eblikpabi zhi uzedhu, zhimu uzedu

3
Me mu Ichakpa uya lor, lu ukaze orbioma
Gbele gbele adhi izhi me ubulor ortizhi
Emene uzhi uma hugbe me,
Eblikpabi zhi uzedu, zhimu uzedu

4
Echiche me teliwe li nina, Bu upadhiwe yo,
Lime eke agbezhi me,
bu uze udhor edhor,
Lu unazhi iwene me
Eblikpabi zhi uzedu, zhimu uzedhu

5
Bule eyi obutor anala me olu, lu ukaze orbioma,
Elanwu adigwe, okpudhor egbuluka zhedhe, me kaze olu
Gbele gbele orbu dhubu
Eblikpabi zhi uzedu, zhimu uzedhu

MH 74   Sweet Hour of Prayer   SDAH 478

William W. Walford, c.1842 (1772-1850)

English

1

Sweet hour of prayer! sweet hour of prayer!
that calls me from a world of care,
and bids me at my Father's throne
make all my wants and wishes known.
In seasons of distress and grief,
my soul has often found relief,
and oft escaped the tempter's snare
by thy return, sweet hour of prayer!

2

Sweet hour of prayer! sweet hour of prayer!
thy wings shall my petition bear
to him whose truth and faithfulness
engage the waiting soul to bless.
And since he bids me seek his face,
believe his word, and trust his grace,
I'll cast on him my every care,
and wait for thee, sweet hour of prayer!

3

Sweet hour of prayer! sweet hour of prayer!
May I thy consolation share
Till from Mount Pisgah's lofty height
I view my home and take my flight.
In my immortal flesh I'll rise
To size the everlasting prize.
And shout while passing through the air,
"Farewell, farewell, sweet hour of prayer!"

MH 74   Sweet Hour of Prayer   SDAH 478

William W. Walford, c.1842 (1772-1850)

Ekpeye Translation

1
Etor ugbe edhor, etor ugbe edhor
Hulorshie me lu uwa usornyenye,
Amu lorwe me la agida eze idame,
Lorwe echiche li iye, makwani uwe.
Leke akwukwu, la agbezhi,
Uwa me weji ushishikeji eka,
Gbele gbele ekele, gbanatu nye egba
leke iyale, Etor ugbe edhor.

2
Etor ugbe edhor, Etor ugbe edhor
Eyi yo, obulawe umekpeli me,
Yo nyi ishushuka lu uwhetu,
Nyo wokwani uwam zhilu seji,
Kporm umeme lu wudhiga upi ya,
Uwetu uka li, utunyizhi ya,
Mo bushi nya, unyeke me,
Me seji yo, Etor ugbe edhor

3
Etor ugbe edhor, Etor ugbe edhor,
Nemu uke lu umawunu ma Yo,
Eke mobuzeli le egbu Pisgah,
Me nyeweji udhor me maba kaze,
Lelim ornwulor ornwulu morlor,
Lu unyeta iye uma ogbo ogbo,
Mechi ikpulu galaga uwukayi
Izeuma, Izeuma, Etor ugbe edhor.

MH 75   I Need Thee Every Hour SDAH 483

Annie S. Hawks, 1872 (1835-1918)

English

1
I need thee every hour,
most gracious Lord;
no tender voice like thine
can peace afford.

Chorus
I need thee, O I need thee;
every hour I need thee;
O bless me now, my Savior, I come to thee.

2
I need thee every hour;
stay thou nearby;
temptations lose their powers,
when thou art nigh.

3
I need thee every hour,
in joy or pain;
come quickly and abide,
or life is vain.

4
I need thee every hour;
teach me thy will;
and thy rich promises
In me fulfill.

MH 75   I Need Thee Every Hour SDAH 483

Annie S. Hawks, 1872 (1835-1918)

Ekpeye Translation

1
Mo wudhiga yo gbele gbele ugbe,
Nyo ortizhi kakpoligbe,
Uzhe uli ka Ayo, Le unedhi uyodhu

Chorus
Mo wudhiga yo, mo wudhiga yo,
Gbele gbele ugbe mo, wudhiga Yo
Wokwanl lumorm, nye nwe me, Mejakeji, lem Yo

2
Mo wudhiga gbele gbele ugbe,
Nazi lu ukwu me
Ugbakpo umama adabada
Layi zhile uzedhu

3
Mo wudhiga yo gbele gbele ugbe
Le obuetor li eli edhe,
Jashi enwa mu inazhi
Eke budu atadhu ewe

4
Mo wudhiga Yo gbele gbele ugbe,
Zhim echiche yo,
Le ogbo, egba uma ma yo le,
Ime me mezu

MH 76   Jesus, Lover of My Soul   SDAH 489

Charles Wesley, 1740 (1707-1788)

English

1
Jesus, lover of my soul,
Let me to Thy bosom fly,
While the nearer waters roll,
While the tempest still is high.
Hide me, O my Savior, hide,
Till the storm of life is past;
Safe into the haven guide;
O receive my soul at last.
2
Other refuge have I none,
Hangs my helpless soul on Thee;
Leave, ah! leave me not alone,
Still support and comfort me.
All my trust on Thee is stayed,
All my help from Thee I bring;
Cover my defenseless head
With the shadow of Thy wing.
3
Thou, O Christ, art all I want,
More than all in Thee I find;
Raise the fallen, cheer the faint,
Heal the sick, and lead the blind.
Just and holy is Thy Name,
I am all unrighteousness.
False and full of sin I am;
Thou art full of truth and grace.

MH 76   Jesus, Lover of My Soul   SDAH 489
Charles Wesley, 1740 (1707-1788)
Ekpeye Translation

1
Jesus nyu ugwushi uwa me,
Whema agbadhu le eka yo,
Leke orwayi nule me,
Leke uwele weshi ike,
Woke mu, nyu ugawe me,
Mu iye budu gamakpo
Nnwe udeli lu udhor ma yo,
Godhu tuhor, uwa me

2
Me nwe mu udor nye nweke me,
Megbe uwa me la eka yo,
Esabete me neten,
Shishi eka mu ikayite mo obu,
Megbe gbele gbele obu me li yo,
Gbele gbele ushishi le me, ma gala
Gbeke ishi me mu akakam,
Lu ukpudhu enye eyi ma yo.

3
Christ bugbo iye mo wudhiga,
Gbele gbele iye zhi li ime ya,
Gbabuze nye dada, uwedhi nye enwu,
Ugwo nye eli udu nye enyekpor
Uma li egwele bu ewa yo
Morbu nye eka ya asusa,
Mo yulu lebiyor li umeyeshi,
Ibu nye ishishuka li ortizhi.

MH 76   Jesus, Lover of My Soul   SDAH 489
Charles Wesley, 1740 (1707-1788)
English

4
Plenteous grace with Thee is found,
Grace to cover all my sin;
Let the healing streams abound;
Make and keep me pure within.
Thou of life the fountain art,
Freely let me take of Thee;
Spring Thou up within my heart;
Rise to all eternity.

MH 76   Jesus, Lover of My Soul   SDAH 489

Charles Wesley, 1740 (1707-1788)

Ekpeye Translation

4
Ibu nye eke ortizhi,
Ortizhi usabetenikpo gbiyor me,
Me mu mini ugwor eli lor,
Meke ume me mozuke,
Ibu mini ne budu,
Memu meke ngonu ewe,
Lowa lime ekpema me,
Dhuma lu ugbe ogbo ogbo

MH 77   What a Friend We Have in Jesus   SDAH 499

James S. Scriven, 1855 (1819-1886)

English

1
What a friend we have in Jesus,
All our sins and griefs to bear!
What a privilege to carry
Everything to God in prayer!
Oh, what peace we often forfeit;
Oh, what needless pain we bear
All because we do not carry
Everything to God in prayer!

2
Have we trials and temptations?
Is there trouble anywhere?
We should never be discouraged
Take it to the Lord in prayer.
Can we find a friend so faithful
Who will all our sorrows share?
Jesus knows our every weakness
Take it to the Lord in prayer.

3
Are we weak and heavy laden,
Cumbered with a load of care?
Precious Savior, still our refuge
Take it to the Lord in prayer.
Do your friends despise, forsake you?
Take it to the Lord in prayer.
In his arms he'll take and shield you;
You will find a solace there.

MH 77   What a Friend We Have in Jesus   SDAH 499

James S. Scriven, 1855 (1819-1886)

Ekpeye Translation

1
Nde uji nuji ya nye le Jesus
Lu ubu gbele gbele umeyeshi ye,
Nde umawunu ye nwe lu ubulawe,
Nyi Eblikpabi edhor ye,
Ubotu uyodhu nali dhiye
Ubotu elidhe ya nye,
Iye dor ya awhe ulawe nyi,
Eblikpabi iye le edhor

2
Ye anwe umama li umekpeli,
Uzhi adhi akwukwu zhi,
Anwe nyi obu udada, laweni Eblikpabi le edhor,
Aweji nwuje enwe uwhetu,
Nyor obu gbele gbele agbezhi ye,
Jesus amajikpole uya ye,
Nedhe Eblikpabi le edhor

3
Abuji ubu li ike ugulu,
Ubu nwedhu una lu ubu,
Nyu ugawe uma ye bu adhi uwoli,
Nedhe Eblikpabi le edhor,
Emene nwuje yo nagbo gbe yo,
Nedhe Eblikpabi le edhor
Lime eka ya owoke yo,
Abadhi ugawe yo zhi

MH 78   Sun of My Soul   SDAH 502
John Keble, 1820 (1792-1866)
English

1
Sun of my soul, O Savior dear!
It is not night if Thou be near;
O may no earth-born cloud arise
To hide Thee from Thy servant's eyes.

2
When soft the dews of kindly sleep
My weary eyelids gently steep,
Be my last thought how sweet to rest
Forever on my Savior's breast!

3
Abide with me from morn till eve,
For without Thee I cannot live;
Abide with me when night is nigh,
For without Thee I dare not die.

4
Be near and bless me when I wake,
Ere through the world my way I take;
Till in the ocean of Thy love
I lose myself in heaven above.

MH 78   Sun of My Soul   SDAH 502
John Keble, 1820 (1792-1866)
Ekpeye Translation

1
Elanwu uwa me, nyu ugawe me,
Ukabor abali lawu zhile uzedhu,
Ewhe gbu igeleni uwa gbuja,
Lu uwoke yo le ekpeleni me

2
Eke etor nina uzhi luja,
Ma abaa ckpeleni ike ugulu ukpudhu,
Bu cchiche me, lc ctor udeli
Gbele gbele ekele le eka nyu ugawe me

3
Nazhi kejim lo oyukwe li ela,
Ubule gbu ezhela ndeke me be dhom,
Nazhi kejim lu uzedhu abali,
Gamale yo ndeke mor nwulorm

4
Zhi uzedhu mi wokwani lu uteli me,
Li ichakpa eluwa bu adhi me ma ga,
Dhuma olimini mu ugwushi ma yo,
Mo owulumalem lime Orbioma

MH 79   Standing on the Promises   SDAH 518

R. Kelso Carter (1849-1928)

English

1
Standing on the promises of Christ my King,
Thru eternal ages let His praises ring;
Glory in the highest I will shout and sing,
Standing on the promises of God.

Chorus
Standing, standing,
Standing on the promises of God my Savior; Standing,
standing,
I'm standing on the promises of God.

2
Standing on the promises that cannot fail,
When the howling storms of doubt and fear assail,
By the living word of God, I shall prevail,
Standing on the promises of God.

3
Standing on the promises of Christ the Lord,
Bound to Him eternally by love's strong cord,
Overcoming daily with the Spirit's sword,
Standing on the promises of God.

MH 79   Standing on the Promises   SDAH 518

R. Kelso Carter (1849-1928)

Ekpeye Translation

1
Mo nuzo lu ugwu egba Christ bu eze me,
Dhuma ugwulu orgwulu upadhi ya udhuzu,
Upadhi kakpoligbe memor whu amgwu
Mo nuzo lu ugwu egba Eblikpabi.

Chorus
Mo nuzo, mo nuzo,
Mo nuzo lu ugwu egba Eblikpabi nyu gawe me,
Mo nuzo, mo nuzo
Mo nuzo le egba Eblikpabi

2
Mo nuzole egba enwe udada,
Leke umama lo otogu jikpudhiegbe me,
Lu unu ekpor Eblikpabi me megbo bu emegbo,
Mo nuzo le egba Eblikpabi

3
Mo nuzo le egba Christ nye nwe ye,
Lu megbedhea lu ugwushi orgwulu gwulu,
Lu ulugbo gbele gbele eye lo oge ulu uwuma,
Mo nuzo le egba mu Eblikpabi

MH 80   It Is Well with My Soul   SDAH 530

Horatio G.Spafford, 1876 (1828-1888)

English

1
When peace, like a river, attendeth my way,
when sorrows like sea billows roll;
whatever my lot, thou hast taught me to say,
It is well, it is well with my soul.

Chorus
It is well with my soul,
it is well, it is well with my soul.

2
My sin--oh, the joy of this glorious thought--
My sin, not in part but the whole,
is nailed to the cross, and I bear it no more,
praise the Lord, praise the Lord, O my soul!

3
And, Lord, haste the day when my faith shall be sight,
the clouds be rolled back as a scroll;
the trump shall resound, and the Lord shall descend,
even so, it is well with my soul.

MH 80   It Is Well with My Soul   SDAH 530

Horatio G.Spafford, 1876 (1828-1888)

Ekpeye Translation

1
Eke uyodhu kporm olimini jale ichakpa me,
Eke agbezhi kporm orwayi nu le me,
Kpulikpu uzhihutor, ye zhileme gbu maka,
Umanu umanunyor bu uwa me!

Chorus
Umanu, nyu uwa me,
Umanu, umanuyi uwa me

2
Umeyeshi me, obu etor echiche upadhi me,
Uzhe li ibe li ibe- uzozu
Kporshi agbe lu ushi uye lu uka, Mobujedhe ma udor,
Padhiwe nye nwe ye, padhiwe nye nwe ye, O uwa me

3
Eye ya jashi enwa, mu uwhetu notua,
Igili onuya gba bu orzu,
Ogbugbe bu ordu, mu nye nwe ye kpeda,
Uzhikpe, Umanunyi uwa me

MH 81   Lord, Dismiss Us with Thy Blessing
SDAH 64

John Fawcett, 1773 (1740-1817)

English

1
Lord, dismiss us with thy blessing;
fill our hearts with joy and peace;
let us each, thy love possessing,
triumph in redeeming grace.
O refresh us, O refresh us,
traveling through this wilderness.

2
Thanks we give and adoration
for thy gospel's joyful sound.
May the fruits of thy salvation
in our hearts and lives abound;
Ever faithful, ever faithful
to the truth may we be found.

MH 81   Lord, Dismiss Us with Thy Blessing
SDAH 64

John Fawcett, 1773 (1740-1817)

Ekpeye Translation
1
Nye nwe ye akaze hor, lu uwokwani yo
Ne ekpema ye obu etor li uyodhu,
Ne nye nyem la ya, ugwushim Ayo,
Utu ugo le ortizhi udorkpewe;
Ba meke ye, bam meke ye,
Lu galaga le ele iwho mu

2
Ya ne Yo ukela li upeni
lu uli uzhi uma obu etor Yo,
Ugawe ma ayo badhu ebala,
Le ekpema li budu ye;
Unuzo lu uwhetu, unuzo lu uwhetu,
Uweji gbeye li ishishuka

MH 82   He Leadeth Me   SDAH 537

J. H. Gilmore, 1862 (1834-1918)

English

1
He leadeth me: O blessed thought!
O words with heavenly comfort fraught!
Whate'er I do, where'er I be,
still 'tis God's hand that leadeth me.

Chorus
He leadeth me, he leadeth me,
by his own hand he leadeth me;
his faithful follower I would be,
for by his hand he leadeth me.

2
Sometimes mid scenes of deepest gloom,
sometimes where Eden's bowers bloom,
by waters still, o'er troubled sea,
still 'tis his hand that leadeth me.

3
Lord, I would place my hand in thine,
nor ever murmur nor repine;
content, whatever lot I see,
since 'tis my God that leadeth me.

4
And when my task on earth is done,
when by thy grace the victory's won,
e'en death's cold wave I will not flee,
since God through Jordan leadeth me.

MH 82   He Leadeth Me   SDAH 537

J. H. Gilmore, 1862 (1834-1918)

Ekpeye Translation

1
Ya bu nye udu me, echiche zhi uwokwani,
Uli ukayita unukwuma orbioma,
Iye li iye me me, adhi li adhi me zhi,
Eka Eblikpabi udu me

Chorus
Ya bu nye udu me, Ya bu nye udu me,
Le eka ma ya udu we me,
Me nwe uwhetu le ichakpa ya,
Le eka mu aya udu we me.

2
Leke igeleni wudhiga uda,
Ladhi upadhi zhillu uzu,
Lime olimini kpadhi iyo
Eka Eblikpabi udu me.

3
Nye nwe ye ma kwashi eka lo yo,
Ndeke ma tabudhe m uka,
Iye li iye me weji ozuni le me,
Kpormu bu Eblikpabi udu me.

4
Eke me mekpo ugbolo me lu uwa,
Lor ortizhi Yo me megbo kpo,
Umashi uwukayi enwu magba natorm,
Kpormu Eblikpabi dulaga me Jordan

MH 83   Guide Me, O Thou Great Jehovah   SDAH 538

William Williams, 1745 (1717-1791)

English

1
Guide me, O thou great Jehovah,
pilgrim through this barren land.
I am weak, but thou art mighty;
hold me with thy powerful hand.
Bread of heaven, bread of heaven,
feed me till I want no more;
feed me till I want no more.

2
Open now the crystal fountain,
whence the healing stream doth flow;
let the fire and cloudy pillar
lead me all my journey through.
Strong deliverer, strong deliverer,
be thou still my strength and shield;
be thou still my strength and shield.

3
When I tread the verge of Jordan,
bid my anxious fears subside;
death of death and hell's destruction,
land me safe on Canaan's side.
Songs of praises, songs of praises,
I will ever give to thee;
I will ever give to thee.

MH 83   Guide Me, O Thou Great Jehovah   SDAH 538

William Williams, 1745 (1717-1791)

Ekpeye Translation

1
Nyeshi kemu enye,Jehovah bu eke,
Dulaga mu le elem ukikem,
Me nwe mu ugbakpo, ibu nye nwe ugbakpo,
Mojike mu le eka ugbakpo Yo,
Gbidhi orbioma, gbi orbioma,
Nedhemu tutu ngwehu udhi,
Nedhemu tutu ngwehu udhi.

2
Kpuma lumorm, udhor mini orbioma,
Adhi mini ugwor eli ugbalorshi,
Me mu echi li ekpulukpu igiligi,
Dume li ize me gbele gbele ekele.
Nye eke ugawe, nye eke ugawe,
Bu nyimu ugbakpo li okpuishi uli
Bu nyimu ugbakpo li okpuishi uli.

3
Eke modhu male, ichakpa Jordan,
Me mu otogu me, ubuzeli,
Enwu li enwu li Udoka uwa gbiyo
Du mu lu uyodhu, dhuma Canaan.
Orbu upadhi, orbu upadhi,
Gbele gbele ekele, morgwuni yo,
Gbele gbele ckele, morgwuni yo.

MH 84 ....We Plow the Fields ....SDAH 561

Matthias Claudius (1740-1815)
Tr. By Jane M. Campbell (1817-1878)
English

1
We plow the fields, and scatter the good seed on the land,
But it is fed and watered by God's almighty hand.
He sends the snow in winter, the warmth to swell the grain,
The breezes and the sunshine, and soft refreshing rain.

Chorus
All good gifts around us
Are sent from heaven above;
Then thank the Lord, O thank the Lord
For all His love.

2
He only is the Maker of all things near and far;
He paints the wayside flower, He lights the evening star.
The winds and waves obey Him, by Him the birds are fed;
Much more, to us His children, He gives our daily bread.

3
We thank Thee then, O Father, for all things bright and good,
The seed-time and the harvest, our life, our health, and food.
Accept the gifts we to offer for all Thy love imparts,
And, what Thou most desirest, our humble, thankful hearts.

MH 84 ....We Plow the Fields ....SDAH 561

Matthias Claudius (1740-1815)
Tr. By Jane M. Campbell (1817-1878)

Ekpeye Translation

1
Ye achi ika mu akpashi ukpulushi le ele,
Une gbidhi li une mini, eka Eblikpabi ne,
Une ukayi lo okidhika, ekechim umewor ukpulishi,
Uwukayi li elanwu, mini udem meke ele

Chorus
Gbele gbele iye umam zhinyor ye,
Buzeli lo orbioma,
Kela nye nwe ye,
Le gbele gbele ugwushi Ya

2
Ya neten bu nye mekpo, gbele gbele iye zhi lu uwa,
Ya yashi agba le ezor ewe, Ya mushi okpudhu egbuluka ela
Uwele li orwayi uyia agbesor, Ya ne ogbo unu gbidhi,
Awu kakpoligbe ye umeledhe Ya, Ya ne ye gbidhi gbele gbele eye.

3
Ya kela Yo, Eda ye gbele gbele iye zorgbe orzor,
Ukpa iye li ugwu ogwu, budu ye eli ike li gbidhi ye,
Natu iye ukela ye agala le gbele gbele ugwushi yo,
Iye wudhiga kakpoligbe bu uyodhu ekpema etor ye.

MH 85   Pass Me Not, O Gentle Savior   SDAH 569

Fanny J. Crosby, 1868 (1820-1915)

English

1
Pass me not, O gentle Savior,
hear my humble cry;
while on others thou art calling,
do not pass me by.

Chorus
Savior, Savior, hear my humble cry;
while on others thou art calling,
do not pass me by.

2
Let me at thy throne of mercy
find a sweet relief,
kneeling there in deep contrition;
help my unbelief.

3
Trusting only in thy merit,
would I seek thy face;
heal my wounded, broken spirit,
save me by thy grace.

4
Thou the spring of all my comfort,
more than life to me,
whom have I on earth beside thee?
Whom in heaven but thee?

MH 85   Pass Me Not, O Gentle Savior   SDAH 569
Fanny J. Crosby, 1868 (1820-1915)
Ekpeye Translation

1
Egama mu nyu ugawe me,
Nuji ekwa me,
Eke izeke jile udor emene,
E ga ma mu

Chorus
Nyu ugawe, Nyu ugawe,Nuji ekwa me,
Leke izeke jile udormene
Ega ma mu

2
La agida eze mu ortizhi Ayo,
Ne me ortizhi Yo
Meji kpunuko lime umeyeshi,
Dor ugwe unwe uwhetu

3
Ugbe unukpuma lor otizhi Yo neten,
Mo wudhiga up Yo,
Gwor umekpeli ime uwa me,
Dormu lor ortizhi Yo

4
Ibu iye ekpema etor me,
Akamale budu,
Nde iye me nwe lu uwa gama Yo,
Lor orbioma bu yo?

MH 86 Trust and Obey   SDAH 590
J. H. Sammis (1846-1919)
English

1
When we walk with the Lord in the light of his word,
what a glory he sheds on our way!
While we do his good will, he abides with us still,
and with all who will trust and obey.

Chorus
Trust and obey, for there's no other way
to be happy in Jesus, but to trust and obey.

2
Not a shadow can rise, not a cloud in the skies,
but his smile quickly drives it away;
not a doubt nor a fear, not a sigh nor a tear,
can abide while we trust and obey.

3
Not a burden we bear, not a sorrow we share,
but our toil he doth richly repay;
not a grief or a loss, not a frown or a cross,
but is blest if we trust and obey.
4
But we never can prove, the delights of his love
until all on the altar we lay;
for the favor he shows, and the joy he bestows,
are for them who will trust and obey.

5
Then in fellowship sweet, we will sit at his feet,
or we'll walk by his side in the way;
what he says we will do, where he sends we will go;
never fear, only trust and obey.

MH 86   Trust and Obey SDAH 590
Ekpeye Translation

1
Eke ye akaze keji nye nwe ye, Le kpeani iye ya,
Nduji obu etor enwe le iye ye,
Eke amale echiche uma ya, Ebor bu le ime ye,
Le ogbo emene gbe to gbe obu li uyi esor

Chorus
Ugbe obu li uyi esor, uzedhe udor ichakpa,
Anye obu etor le Jesus, ugama ugbe obu li uyi esor

2
Uzhe enye orlordho, Uzhe igiligi lo olu,
Umuya echimakpo enwe nwa,
Uzhe unyodhe enye li otogu,
Uzhe uta uta li ekwa,
Ezhi dho leke agbele obu li esor

3
Uzhe eke ubu ubuji,
Uzhe agbezhi ye agba,
Ugbolo ye orhor ye ugwu uma,
Uzhe akwukwu li uwulu,
Uzhe ushi upi li ushi uye li uka,
Gama uwokwani lawu agbele obu li uyi esor

4
Ndeke ye akalorshie dho kpu ugwushi Ya zhile,
Gama agbe gbele gbele iye ladhi orsor eja,
Le uwhe uka uwheni ye,
Le ekpe ma etor unedhi,
Bu awu emene gbe gbe obu li uyi esor.
5
Le etor uchi dhiga, Anazhor bu ezhi lu uko ya,
Ma akadhe lu ukwu eli ya le ichakpa,
Iye uka bu iye ame, Adhi uzhile bu adhi aze,
Etogwu gbehutor obu li uyi esor.

MH 87   Christian, Seek Not Repose   SDAH 603

Charlotte Elliot, 1839 (1789-1871)

English

1
Christian, seek not yet repose,
Cast thy dreams of ease away;
Thou art in the midst of foes;
Watch and pray!

2
Gird thy heavenly armor on,
Wear it ever, night and day;
Ambushed lies the evil one;
Watch and pray!

3
Hear the victors who o'er came;
Still they mark each warrior's way;
All with one sweet voice exclaim: "Watch and pray!"

4
Hear, above all, hear thy Lord,
Him thou lovest to obey;
Hide within thy heart His word; "Watch and pray!"

5
Watch, as if on that alone
Hung the issue of the day;
Pray that help may be send down; Watch and pray!

MH 87   Christian, Seek Not Repose   SDAH 603

Charlotte Elliot, 1839 (1789-1871)

Ekpeye Translation

1
Emene Christ enyeni nyina,
Namanyi budu orgborgor Yo,
Izhini li ime emene egba,
Seji mi edhor!

2
Nyaji oge ulu orbioma yo,
Nyadhiga li abali li eye
Nye gbiyor dhuwoli lime uya,
Seji mi edhor!

3
Nuji nyu umegbo kpu umegbole,
Uzhi lu wu ejigbe ichakpa ulu,
Gbele gbele gbe kagbe li uli etor,
"Seji mi edhor!"

4
Nuji, awu kakpoligbe, nujini nye nwe yo,
Nye mu uwheshor gbi iyi esor,
Woke ekpema le ekpor Ya,
"Seji mi edhor!"

5
Seji gbu bukwa ya neten,
Bu iyeme li eye ya,
Dhor mu uyewegbe ushishi eka,
Seji mi edhor!

MH 88 The Wise May Bring their Learning SDAH 638

Book of Praise for Children, 1881

English

1
The wise may bring their learning,
The rich may bring their wealth,
And some may bring their greatness,
And some their strength and health:
We too would bring our treasures
To offer to the King,
We have no wealth or learning
What shall we children bring?

2
We'll bring Him hearts that love Him,
We'll bring Him thankful praise,
And young souls meekly striving
To follow in His ways:
And these be the treasures
We offer to the King,
And these are gifts that ever
The poorest child may bring.

3
We'll bring the little duties
We have to do each day;
We'll try our best to please Him
At home, at school, at play:
And better are these treasures
To offer to the King
Than richest gift without them:
Yet these a child may bring.

MH 88 The Wise May Bring their Learning SDAH 638

Book of Praise for Children, 1881

Ekpeye Translation

1
Emene umajiye galagbe iye umudhigbe,
Emene eze galagbe ekpe gbe,
Ubotu agalagbe orgilinya gbe,
Ubotu agalagbe ugbakpo gbe,
Ye dhilu agala iye uma ye,
Lu nedhe eze ya,
Ye anwe ekpe li umuweji,
Ndc iyc umeledhe agala

2
Ye agala ekpema mu ugwushi la,
Ye agala upadhi umeledhe uludhiga gbe lu uyodhu,
Lu uchize ichakpa Ya,
Ombu iye umam aye, ya nedhe eze ye,
Ombu iye uke gbele gbele ekele,
Umeledhe ogboyi agalagbe.

3
Ye agala ugbolo ntukor,
Ame le gbele gbele eye,
Agbake mu ekpema tua etor
Lu udhor, ladhi umudhi li unama,
Iye ka uma bu ogbo iye uma mu anedhe eze ye
Ka iye ugbu ayo, amu orbor iye uma
Ombu iye umeledhe agalagbe

MH 89   Onward, Christian Soldiers!   SDAH 612

Sabine Baring-Gould, 1864

English

1
Onward, Christian soldiers, marching as to war,
with the cross of Jesus going on before.
Christ, the royal Master, leads against the foe;
forward into battle see his banners go!

Chorus
Onward, Christian soldiers, marching as to war,
with the cross of Jesus going on before.

2
Like a mighty army moves the church of God;
brothers, we are treading where the saints have trod.
We are not divided, all one body we,
one in hope and doctrine, one in charity.

3
Crowns and thrones my perish, kingdoms rise and wane,
but the church of Jesus constant will remain.
Gates of hell can never 'gainst that church prevail;
we have Christ's own promise, and that cannot fail.

4
Onward then, ye people, join our happy throng,
blend with ours your voices in the triumph song.
Glory, laud, and honor unto Christ the King,
this through countless ages men and angels sing.

MH 89   Onward, Christian Soldiers!   SDAH
612
Sabine Baring-Gould, 1864
Ekpeye Translation

1
Kazenyi emene ulu Jesus, kazenyi luze ulu,
Lu ushi uye li uka Jesus, Ukaze lu ununu,
Christ eze edan wudhor ye, Orlugbo nyiye nye egba,
Kaze, dhuma adhi ulu weji iye eji udhu kaze

Chorus
Kazenyi emene ulu Jesus,
kazenyi kpormu uze ulu,
Ushi uye li uke Jesus
Kaze lu ununu

2
Kpormu eke emene ulu
Uunu uzugbani Eblikpabi,
Emene Christ ye azorji uko
Adhi emene uzhi uma zorjigbe,
Uzhe ukema le ime ya, gbele gbele ye abu unwune,
Unwune le uwhetu, unwune lu ukpa agwa.
3
Okpulishi li agida eze tadhu gbe,
Emene zhigbe lulor zhigbe luda,
Uzugban mu Jesus, onuzo dhe bu kpe.
Egbeleta uwa gbiyo unwe ugbakpo,
Lu utashi uzugbani ya, Ya anwe egba,
Christ gwunyi ye, Ya ndeke egwu ume
4
Kazenyi ogbo emene madu Kpudhunyi lime ogbo mu aye,
Shishini ni ye uli ma yo, Lorbu umegbo ma aye,
Esor, upadhi li utubuze, Zhini Christ bu Eze,
Ombu iye, zhili ukanyi, orbu emene uzhi uma gwugbe.

MH 90   Come Thou Almighty King   SDAH 71

Annon. Hymns for Social Worship, 1757

English

1
Come, Thou almighty King,
Help us Thy name to sing,
Help us to praise!
Father all glorious, O'er all victorious,
Come, and reign over us,
Ancient of Days!

2
Come, Thou incarnate Word,
Gird on Thy mighty sword,
Our prayer attend;
Come, and Thy people bless,
And give Thy Word success;
Spirit of holiness, on us descend!

3
Come, holy cmforter,
Thy sacred witness bear,
In this glad hour,
Thou who almighty art,
Now rule on every heart,
And never from us depart, Spirit of power

4
To Thee, great One in Three,
Eternal praises be,
Hence, evermore:
Thy sovereign majesty
May we in glory see, And to eternity
Love and adore!

MH 90 Come   Thou Almighty King   SDAH 71
Annon. Hymns for Social Worship, 1757
Ekpeye Translation

1
Ja, Eze kakpoligbe,
Shishi eka lu ugbabuze ewa Yo,
Shishi eka lu upadhiwe Yo,
Eda gbele gbele ugo,
Le gbele gbele umegbo,
Ja, meke ichi ye, nye zhili ukani

2
Ja, uli ekpor zhili madu,
Nyaji oge ulu ma Ayo,
Nuji edhor ye, Ja, mi wokwani emene Yo,
Me ekpor yo kaze ununu,
Uwa egwele ja keji ye

3
Ja, uwuma ukayite uma,
Gba ekibo egwele mu Ayo,
Lu ugbe obu etor, Ibu iye kakpoligbe,
Lumorm, chigbele gbele ekpema,
Ebuzele le eli ye, uwuma ugbakpo.

4
Yo, eke unwune li gbitor,
Izhi lu upadhi ogbo ogbo,
Inwe ugbo ogbo,
Unazhi eze aliye Yo,
Me mu aweja le esor,
Dhuma eke ogbo ogbo, ugwushi li ukpeni

MH 91 Let Us with a Gladsome Mind SDAH 112

John Milton, 1623 (1608-1674)

English

1
Let us with a gladsome mind
Praise the Lord, for He is kind:
For His mercies shall endure,
Ever faithful, ever sure.

2
He, with all-commanding might,
Filled the new-made world with light:
For His mercies shall endure,
Ever faithful, ever sure.

3
All things living He does feed;
His full hand supplies their need:
For His mercies shall endure,
Ever faithful, ever sure.

4
Let us then with gladsome mind
Praise the Lord, for He is kind:
For His mercies shall endure,
Ever faithful, ever sure.

MH 91   Let Us with a Gladsome Mind   SDAH 112

John Milton, 1623 (1608-1674)

Ekpeye Translation

1
Jani ma zhi le ekpema etor,
Kela Eblikpabi, le egwuma Ya,
Ortizhi ya ugwulu orgwulu,
Uwhetu ya zhidhi kpe.

2
Lu ugbakpo zhili utuka ya,
Unedihe eluwa uwu usamali,
Ortizhi ya ugwulu orgwulu,
Uwhetu ya zhidhi kpe.

3
Iye zhigbe budu ya ne gbidhi,
Eka ya niye uwudhiga gbe,
Ortizhi ya ugwulu orgwulu,
Uwhetu ya zhidhi kpe.

4
Jani, ma zhi le ekpema etor,
Kela Eblikpabi li egwuma Ya,
Ortizhi ya ugwulu orgwulu,
Uwhetu ya zhidhi kpe.

MH 92   O Come, All Ye Faithful   SDAH 132

Annon. Latin 18th Century

English

1
O come, all ye faithful,
Joyful and triumphant,
O come ye, O come ye to Bethlehem!
Come and behold Him,
Born the King of angels!

Chorus
O come, let us adore Him,
O come, let us adore Him,
O come, let us adore Him,
Christ, the Lord!
2
Sing, choirs of angels,
Sing in exultation,
O sing, all ye citizens of heaven above!
Glory to God, all glory in the highest!

3
Yea, Lord, we greet Thee,
Born this happy morning,
Jesus, to Thee be all glory given;
Word of the Father,
Now in flesh appearing!

MH 92   O Come, All Ye Faithful   SDAH 132

Annon. Latin 18th Century

Ekpeye Translation

1
Jani emene uwhetu,
le obu etor lu ulor ugo,
Jani, jani le Bethelehem,
Ja ma padhiwani,
Umugbe eze uzhi uma.

Chorus
Jani, meke akpenya nyi,
Jani, meke akpenya nyi,
Jani, meke akpenya nyi.
Christ bu Nye nwe ye.

2
Gwuni emene orbu uzhi uma,
Gwuni le utubuza olu,
Gwuni gbele gbele emene
Zhini lor orbioma,
Esor zhini Eblikpabi,
gbele gbele esor kakpoligbe.

3
Nye nwe ye, ya kela yo ,
Umuagbe le oyukwe upadhi,
Jesus ane Yo gbele gbele esor,
Uli ekpor Eda
ye ulorhor, le orkpeli upata

MH 93 Silent Night, Holy Night SDAH 143

Joseph Mohr, 1818 (1792-1848)

English

1
Silent night, holy night,
All is calm, all is bright;
Round yon virgin mother and Child!
Holy Infant, so tender and mild,
Sleep in heavenly peace,
Sleep in heavenly peace.
2
Silent night, holy night,
Darkness flies, all is light;
Shepherds hear the angels sing,
"Alleluia! Hail the King!
Christ the Saviour is born,
Christ the Saviour is born."
3
Silent night, holy night,
Son of God, love's pure light;
Radiant beams from Thy holy face,
With the dawn of redeeming grace,
Jesus, Lord, at Thy birth,
Jesus, Lord, at Thy birth.
4
Silent night, holy night,
Wondrous star, lend thy light;
With the angels let us sing,
Alleluia to our King;
Christ the Saviour is born,
Christ the Saviour is born.

MH 93   Silent Night, Holy Night   SDAH 143

Joseph Mohr, 1818 (1792-1848)

Ekpeye Translation

1
Abali ugwe ekpor, abali zhi egwele,
Adhi zhi orgwor eji, adhi unyudhi,
Ushikoshi Yo nwu ugbedhe ena li unwor,
Unwor zhi egwele li odhu esor,
Nyinina uyodhu orbioma,
Nyinina uyodhu orbioma.

2
Abali ugwe ekpo, abali zhi egwele,
Igeleni gba esor, adhi samali,
Emene udu ornor nujigbe
Orbu emene uzhi uma,
Al-le-lu-ia gwunibe Eze zhi esor,
Ormulegbe Christ nyu gawe ye,
Ormulegbe Christ nyu gawe ye.

3
Abali ugwe ekpor, abali zhi egwele,
Unwor Eblikpabi, ugwushi usamali,
Unyumali buzeli lu upi zhi egwele,
Lu ujeja ortizhi udorkpeye,
Jesus, Nyu gawe, lu umu Yo,
Jesus, Nyu gawe, lu umu Yo.

4
Abali ugwu ekpor, abali zhi egwele,
Orkpudhor egbuluka tudhigbe otogu mushigbe echigbe,
Ye li emene uzhi uma agwuni orbu,
Al-le-lu-ia ma nwenyi Eze ye,
Ormulegbe Christ nyu gawe ye,
Ormulegbe Christ nyu gawe ye.

MH 94   Christ the Lord Is Risen Today   SDAH 166
Charles Wesley, 1739, (1707-1788)
English

1
Christ the Lord is risen today, Alleluia!
Sons of men and angels say, Alleluia!
Raise your joys and triumphs high, Alleluia!
Sing, ye heavens, and earth reply, Alleluia!

2
Lives again our glorious King, Alleluia!
Where, O death, is now thy sting? Alleluia!
Once He died, our souls to save, Alleluia!
Where's thy victory, boasting grave? Alleluia!

3
Love's redeeming work is done, Alleluia!
Fought the fight, the battle won, Alleluia!
Death in vain forbids Him rise, Alleluia!
Christ hath opened Paradise, Alleluia!

4
Soar we then where Christ has led, Alleluia!
Following our exalted Head, Alleluia!
Made like Him, like Him we rise, Alleluia!
Ours the cross, the grave, the skies, Alleluia!

MH 94   Christ the Lord Is Risen Today   SDAH 166
Charles Wesley, 1739, (1707-1788)
Ekpeye Translation

1
Christ nye nwe de le li tam, Al-le-lu-ia,
Umu madu li emene uzhi uma kani , Al-le-lu-ia,
Gbuzeni obuetor li ugo Yo olu, Al-le-lu-ia,
Emene orbioma gwuni, Eluwa sani, Al-le-lu-ia!

2
Ezhi gbale, Eze esor ye, Al-le-lu-ia,
Enwu nde ugbakpo yo lu morm? Al-le-lu-ia,
Unwulu mu udorkpewe ye, Al-lc-lu-ia,
Nde ugbakpo ili nyi ide? Al-le lu-ia!

3
Emele ugolo ugwushi ugawe, Al-le-lu-ia,
Orlule ulu emegbole,Al-le-lu-ia,
Enwu umedho meke ugwe ule, Al-le-lu-ia,
Christ okpumale ele eze, Al-le-lu-ia!

4
Ukaze olu bu adhi Jesus dulaye ye, Al-le-lu-ia,
Achize nyishiali ye mu aye, Al-le-lu-ia,
Umegbe ye kpormu Ya, kpormu Ya ye ale, Al-le-lu-ia,
Aye bu ushi uye li uka ili li olu, Al-le-lu-ia!

MH 95 Spirit of the Living God SDAH 672
Daniel Iverson, 1926 (1890-1977)
English

Spirit of the living God,
Fall afresh on me!
Spirit of the living God,
Fall afresh on me!
Break me, melt me, mold me, fill me!
Spirit of the living God,
Fall afresh on me!

MH 95 Spirit of the Living God SDAH 672
Daniel Iverson, 1926 (1890-1977)
Ekpeye Translation

Uwa mu Eblikpabi zhi,
Ibudum daa lime me,
Uwa mu Eblikpabi zhi,
Ibudum daa lime me,
Dorkam, nwagbazam, kpumu, shishikem,
Uwa mu Eblikpabi zhi,
Ibudum daa lime me.

MH 96   Praise God, From Whom All Blessings..
SDAH 694

Thomas Ken, 1695 (1637-1710)

English

Praise God, from Whom all blessings flow;
Praise Him, all creatures here below;
Praise Him above, ye heavenly host;
Praise Father, Son, and Holy Ghost.

MH 96 Praise God, From Whom All Blessings..
SDAH 694

Thomas Ken, 1695 (1637-1710)

Ekpeye Translation

Padhiwe Eblikpabi nye gala uwokwani
Padhiwe gbele gbele iye ukpu le eluwa,
Padiwe nyi le olu emene orbioma,
Padhiwe Eda, le unworn le uwa zhi
egwele.

MH 97 Go, Tell It on the Mountain SDAH 121

American Negro Spiritual

English

Chorus
Go, tell it on the mountain,
Over the hills and everywhere:
Go, tell it on the mountain
That Jesus Christ is born!

1
While shepherds kept their watching
O'er silent flocks by night,
Behold throughout the heavens
There shone a holy light.

2
The shepherds feared and trembled
When lo! Above the earth
Rang out the angel chorus
That hailed our Savior's birth.

3
Down in a lowly manger
The humble Christ was born,
And brought us God's salvation
That blessed Christmas morn.

MH 97 Go, Tell It on the Mountain SDAH 121

American Negro Spiritual

Ekpeye Translation

Chorus
Ze, kalani le olu egbu,
Le olu egbu li gbele gbele adhi
Ze, kalani le olu egbu,
Gbu ormulegbe Jesus Christ

1
Kpormu emene udu ornor
zhigbc lu useji,
Ornor gbe li abali,
Weji gbele gbele orbioma,
kpu unyumali le egwele.

2
Emene udu ornor tugbe otogu mu uhudhi gbe,
Leke akpete le eluwa,
Emene uzhi uma orgwule gbe orbu,
Lu gbabuze umu nyu ugawe.

3
Li ime ukpor gbidhi ornor,
Umugbe Christ umam,
Nye gala ye ugawe Eblikpabi,
Le uwokwani oyukwe christmas.

MH 98 While Shepherds Watched Their Flocks
SDAH 139

Nahum Tate, 1700 (1652-1715)

English

1
While shepherds watched their flocks by night,
All seated on the ground,
The angel of the Lord came down,
And glory shone around

2
"Fear not!" said he – for mighty dread
Had seized their troubled mind –
"Glad tidings of great joy I bring,
To you and all mankind.

3
"To you, in David's town this day,
Is born of David's line,
The Saviour who is Christ the Lord;
And this shall be the sign:

4
"The heavenly Babe you there shall find
To human view displayed,
All meanly wrapped in swathing bands,
And in a manger laid."

5
Thus spake the seraph; and forthwith
Appeared a shining throng
Of angels praising God on high,
Who thus addressed their song:

6
"All glory be to God on high,
And to the earth be peace;
Good will henceforth from heaven to men,
Begin and never cease!"

MH 98 While Shepherds Watched Their Flocks
SDAH 139

Nahum Tate, 1700 (1652-1715)

Ekpeye Translation

1
Emene udu ugaga segbe ornor la abali,
Gbele gbelem nazhigbe le ele,
Eme ushi uma nye nwe ye kpedagbe,
Igili nwukoshi adhi.
2
Etorni otogu le eke iye mu,
Mekpa unukwuma yo eli,
Ma gala uku uma torwe eke ekpema,
Yo le gbele gbele emene uma.
3
Le ime ula David le tam,
Umu nyi gbe ye unwor,
Nyu ugawe bu Christ nye nwe ye,
Ombu iye ugbushi eji.
4
Unwor orbioma me ewejorni,
Ulor li uzazhi madu,
Ugbugbashi kpo agbe lu ukani unwor,
Nyite agbe lu ukpor gbidhi unwor.
5
Kpormu nyu uzhi uma kama hutor,
Ogbo emene nyudhigbe orlolegbe.
Emene uzhi uma padhiwe gbe Eblikpabi,
Nye mu nator orbugbe.
6
Esor zhini Eblikpabi lo olu,
Uyodhu zhi le Eluwa,
Ehiche uma orbioma zhini madu,
Lu umorm dhuma eke ogbo ogbo.

MH 99   When the Roll Is Called Up Yonder SDAH 216

J. M. Black (1856-1938)

English

1
When the trumpet of the Lord shall sound, and time shall be no more,
And the morning breaks eternal, bright and fair;
When the saved of earth shall gather over on the other shore,
And the roll is called up yonder, I'll be there.

Chorus
When the roll is called up yonder,
When the roll is called up yonder,
When the roll is called up yonder,
When the roll is called up yonder,
I'll be there.

2
On that bright and cloudless morning, when the dead in Christ shall rise,
And the glory of His resurrection share;
When His chosen ones shall gather to their home beyond the skies,
And the roll is called up yonder, I'll be there.

3
Let us labour for the Master from the dawn till setting sun,
Let us talk of all His wondrous love and care,
Then, when all of life is over, and our work on earth is done.
And the roll is called up yonder, I'll be there.

MH 99   When the Roll Is Called Up Yonder SDAH 216

J. M. Black (1856-1938)

Ekpeye Translation

1
Eke ordu nye nwe ye kporle,
Mu ugbe gwehor zhidho gba,
Mu oyukwe lorgbo mahorle, lu uzorzor,
Emene ugawe eluwa kpogbani gbe,
lorzu olimini, mu uhwu gbewa ,
Mezhor bu ladhi ya.

Chorus
Uhwule gbe ewa, la adhi ya,
Uhwule gbe ewa, la adhi ya,
Uhwule gbe ewa, la adhi ya,
Uhwule gbe ewa mezhor bu la adhi ya.
3
La usamali oyukwe igiligi ezhe,
Emene enwu CChrist ele gbe,
Enye uke lu ule le enwu, esor mu aya,
Eke emene ulor tugbe agba gbonigbe,
lu udhor gbe lime orbioma,
Mu ugbe ewa mezhor bu, la adhi ya

3
Amenyi Edanwudhor ye ugbolo
gonu lo oyuke dhuma ela,
Akani ugwushi li unyeke Ya,
Iye kpani budu ugwulu kpo le,
Ma mekpo ugbolo ye lu uwa,
Mu uhwe gbe ewa mezhor bu la adhi ya.

MH 100   Whiter Than Snow   SDAH 318

James Nicholson, 1872 (1828-1876)

English

1
Lord Jesus, I long to be perfectly whole;
I want Thee forever to live in my soul;
Break down every idol, cast out every foe;
Now wash me, and I shall be whiter than snow.

Chorus
Whiter than snow, yes, whiter than snow;
Now wash me, and I shall be whiter than snow.

2
Lord Jesus, look down from Thy throne in the skies,
And help me to make a complete sacrifice;
I give up myself, and whatever I know;
Now wash me, and I shall be whiter than snow

3
Lord Jesus, for this I most humbly entreat;
I wait, blessed Lord, at Thy crucified feet,
By faith, for my cleansing; I see Thy blood flow;
Now wash me, and I shall be whiter than snow.

4
Lord Jesus, Thou seest I patiently wait;
Come now, and within me a new heart create;
To those who have sought Thee,
Thou never said'st No;
Now wash me, and I shall be whiter than snow.

MH 100   Whiter Than Snow   SDAH 318

James Nicholson, 1872 (1828-1876)

Ekpeye Translation

1
Jesus, mo wudhiga meke nzuke,
Mo wudhiga mibe lime uwa me,
Namakpo uwa gbiyo, chima emene egba,
Samam mu saka mini orkpor eligwe.

Chorus
Nsaka, mini orkpor eligwe,
Nsaka, mini orkpor eligwe,
Samam mu nsaka, mini orkpor eligwe.

2
Jesus nye dawu enye la agida eze ma Yo,
Mi shishi eka meke morsor eja zuke,
Mene elime lo ogbo iye ma maji,
Samam mu nsaka, mini orkpor eligwe.

3
Jesus, ombu iye mordhor shiyo ike,
Me seji Eda uwokwani lu ukom ukpor gbe egborm,
Lu uwhetu me weji ubala kpu ugbale,
Samam mu nsaka mini orkpor eligwe.

4
Jesus, iweji kpume seji lor orgweji,
Ja, mishishi mu ekpema awu uwu,
Emene wudhiga Yo, uweji Yo,
Samam, nsaka, mini orkpor eligwe.

MH 101   The Strife Is O'er SDAH 172

Tr. By Francis Pott (1832-1909)

English

1
Alleluia, alleluia, alleluia!
The strife is o'er, the battle done;
Now is the victor's triumph won!
Now be the song of praise begun.
Alleluia!

2
The pow'rs of death have done their worst,
But Christ their legions has dispersed.
Let shouts of holy joy outburst.
Alleluia!

3
The three sad days have quickly sped,
He rises glorious from the dead.
All glory to our risen head!
Alleluia!

4
Lord, by the stripes which wounded You,
From death's sting free Your servants too,
That we may live and sing to You.
Alleluia!

MH 101   The Strife Is O'er SDAH 172
Tr. By Francis Pott (1832-1909)
Ekpeye Translation

1
Al-le-lu-ia, Al-le-lu-ia, Al-le-lu-ia!
Edhi ogbole, ulu orgwulule,
Lu morm nyu umegbo otule ugo,
Orbu upadhi odhumale lumorm.
Al-le-lu-ia!

2
Ugbakpo enwu emekpole iye ume,
Emene ulu Christ echimakpo le gbe,
Jani ma achi ikpu obu etor egwele.
Al-le-lu-ia!

3
Eye agbezhi agakpole gbe,
Ele le lu ugole enwu,
Upadhi bawu nyi ishi mu ule nyor ye.
Al-le-lu-ia!

4
Nye nwe ye egbani egbanim umedhu ma Yo elim,
Emene uzhi Yo obuzeli dhehule gbe le enwu,
Meke azhi magwuni Yo orbu
Al-le-lu-ia!

MH 102   Showers of Blessing   SDAH 195

Daniel W. Whittle (1840-1901)

English

1
"There shall be showers of blessing;"
This is the promise of love;
There shall be seasons refreshing,
Sent from the Saviour above.

Chorus
Showers of blessing,
(Showers, showers of blessing,)
Showers of blessing we need;
Mercy drops rounds us are falling,
But for the showers we plead.

2
"There shall be showers of blessing-"
Precious reviving again;
Over the hills and the valleys,
Sound of abundance of rain.

3
"There shall be showers of blessing;"
Send them upon us, O Lord;
Grant to us now a refreshing;
Come, and now honour Thy word.

4
"There shall be showers of blessing;"
O that today they might fall,
Now as to God we're confessing,
Now as on Jesus we call!

MH 102   Showers of Blessing   SDAH 195
Daniel W. Whittle (1840-1901)
Ekpeye Translation

1
Uwokwani orwuda bu orwuda,
Ombu egba ugwushi,
Ezhor bu ugbe umeke iye,
Uja le eka nyu ugawe ye

Chorus
Uwuda uwokwani,
Uwuda uwokwani bu iye adhor,
Ortizhim dakoshi ye adalegbe,
Uwuda uwokwani bu iye ye adhor.

2
Uwokwani orwuda bu orwuda,
Mu iye uma jiosali orzu,
Le olu egbu li ime idagu,
Ekpor eke mini dede.

3
Uwokwani orwuda bu orwuda,
Zhigala nyiye nye nwe ye,
Neye awu uwu lu umormu,
Ja, mu ebamezu ekpor yo.

4
Uwokwani orwuda bu orwuda
Uda mahorgbe li tam,
Ya akani Eblikpabi umeyeshi ye,
Kpormu umorm ye ahor Jesus.

MH 103 Look, You Saints! the Sight Is Glorious
SDAH 165
Thomas Kelly (1769-1854)
English

1
Look, you saints, the sight is glorious,
 See the Man of sorrows now;
From the fight returned victorious,
Every knee to Him shall bow.
Crown Him! Crown Him! Crown Him!
Crown Him! Crown Him! Crown Him!
Crowns become the victor's brow.
 Crowns become the victor's brow.

2
Crown the Saviour! angels crown Him!
Rich the trophies Jesus brings;
On the seat of power enthrone Him
While the vault of heaven rings.
Crown Him! Crown Him! Crown Him!
Crown Him! Crown Him! Crown Him!
Crown the Saviour, King of kings.
Crown the Saviour, King of kings.

3
Sinners in derision crowned Him,
Mocking thus the Saviour's claim;
Saints and angels crowd around Him,
Own His title, praise His name.
Crown Him! Crown Him! Crown Him!
Crown Him! Crown Him! Crown Him!
Spread abroad the victor's fame!
Spread abroad the victor's fame!

MH 103 Look, You Saints! the Sight Is Glorious
SDAH 165
Thomas Kelly (1769-1854)
Ekpeye Translation

1
Emene uzhi uma notuni, kpadhi zule,
Weji nye agbezhi le umorm, Uya lu ulu emegbole,
Gbele gbele ukpunuko ujinya agbe.
Mewani eze! mewani eze! Mewani eze!
Mewani eze! mewani eze! Mewani eze!
Umewe eze uhweshi nyc megbo,
Umewe eze uhweshi nye megbo.

2
Nyu ugawe bu eze, emene uzhi uma mewani,
Jesus gala iye eji umegbo, la agida ugbakpo,
nazhi petanyi, Me emene orbioma padhigbe.
Mewani eze, mewani eze,
Meweni nyu ugawe eze ka eze,
Mewani eze, mewani eze,
Meweni nyu ugawe eze ka eze.

3
Emene umeyeshi, lime iwene ukpadhiwe agbe,
Kpadhiweni nyu ugawe,
Emene uzhi uma shikoshi ani,
Hwetu nyi ani padhiwe ewa Ya.
Mewani eze, mewani eze,
Kakoshini ewa nyu umegbo,
Mewani eze, mewani eze,
Kakoshini ewa nyu umegbo.

MH 103 Look, You Saints! the Sight Is Glorious
SDAH 165
Thomas Kelly (1769-1854)
English

4.
Hark! Those burst of acclamation, hark!
Those loud triumphant chords
Jesus takes the highest station
Oh, what joy that sight affords,
Crown Him! Crown Him! Crown Him!
Crown Him! Crown Him! Crown Him!
Crown Him King of Kings and Lord of Lords.

MH 103 Look, You Saints! the Sight Is Glorious
SDAH 165
Thomas Kelly (1769-1854)
Ekpeye Translation

4

Nujini uwhu, emene natugbe nujini,
Ikpu ugo nye megbo,
Jesus gonu unazhi kakpoligbe,
Ndekpu obu etor ya ezhile.
Mewani eze, mewani eze
Mewani eze ka eze li nye nwe ye,
Mewani eze, mewani eze
Mewani eze ka eze li nye nwe ye.

MH 104   Be Still, My Soul   SDAH 461

Kathrina vn Schlegel, 1752 (1697-)
Tr. By Jane Borthwick, 1855 (1813-1897)
English

1
Be still, my soul: the Lord is on thy side;
bear patiently the cross of grief or pain;
leave to thy God to order and provide;
in every change he faithful will remain.
Be still, my soul: thy best, thy heavenly Friend
through thorny ways leads to a joyful end.

2
Be still, my soul: thy God doth undertake
to guide the future as he has the past.
Thy hope, thy confidence let nothing shake;
all now mysterious shall be bright at last.
Be still, my soul: the waves and winds still know
his voice who ruled them while he dwelt below.

3

Be still, my soul:
the hour is hastening on
When we shall be forever with the Lord,
When disappointment, grief, and fear are gone,
Sorrow forgot, love's purest joys restored.
Be still, my soul: when change and tears are past,
All safe and blessed we shall meet at last.

MH 104   Be Still, My Soul   SDAH 461

Kathrina vn Schlegel, 1752 (1697-)
Tr. By Jane Borthwick, 1855 (1813-1897)
Ekpeye Translation

1
Uwa me yodhu, Nye nwe ye dhula keji yo,
Kayi teku uma, ushi uye li uka agbezhi li idhe,
Gbem Eblikpabi, mu uka ugala
Gbele gbele ugbanyo ezhor lu uku eliyo,
Uwa me yodhu eke nwuje
Oribioma yo, lo okpe ugwu
Odulawe yo lu obu etor.

2
Uwa me yodhu, Eblikpabi ogonu
Lu meke ununu, kpormu umekor ugbegaga
Unye enye lu ugbe obu ezhe
Iye ugbanya-a ogbo akwukwum orgwulor bu
Orgwulu uwa me yodhu
Orwayi li uwele majigbe
Uli nye echi adhi mu ubogbe.

3

Uwa me yodhu, ekele kpor enwe enwe,
Eke anazhi torwu ume ye li nye new ye
Eke unagbo, agbezhi li otogu orgwulor,
Agbezhi gama, ugwushi lu obu etor uzhigba,
Uwa me yodhu, eke ugbanyo,
Uwa me yodhu, eke ugbanyo li ekwa agakpor,
Budu li uwokwani zhini ye

MH 105   God Be With You   SDAH 65

Jeremiah E. Rankin, 1880 (1828-1904)

English

1
God be with you till we meet again;
By His counsels guide, uphold you,
With His sheep securely fold you;
God be with you till we meet again.

Chorus
Till we meet, till we meet,
Till we meet at Jesus' feet;
Till we meet, till we meet,
God be with you till we meet again.

2
God be with you till we meet again;
'Neath His wings securely hide you;
Daily manna still provide you;
God be with you till we meet again.

3
God be with you till we meet again;
When life's perils thick confound you;
Put His arms unfailing round you;
God be with you till we meet again.

4
God be with you till we meet again;
Keep love's banner floating over you,
Strike death's threatening wave before you;
God be with you till we meet again.

MH 105   God Be With You   SDAH 65

Jeremiah E. Rankin, 1880 (1828-1904)

Ekpeye Translation

1
Eblikpabi zhikeji yo dhuma awejita udor,
Lu umaji iye Ya, umojike yo,
Lu unyeshi enye ya, uwoke ke yo,
Eblikpabi zhikeji yo mawejita udor

Chorus
Mawejita, mawejita, mawejita gba udor,
Mawejita lu uko Jesus
Mawejita, mawejita, mawejita gba udor,
Eblikpabi zhikeji yo dhuma awejita udor

2
Eblikpabi zhikeji yo dhuma awejita udor,
Ukpudhu eyi ya uwoke yo,
Une yo gbidhi gbele gbele eye,
Eblikpabi zhikeji yo mawejita udor
3
Eblikpabi zhikeji yo dhuma awejita udor,
Eke budu kike kpupidhe yo,
Uwhakoshi yo eka, ugawe mu aya,
Eblikpabi zhikeji yo dhuma awejita udor.

4
Eblikpabi zhikeji yo dhuma awejita udor,
Gbe iye eji ugwushi mu ushidhiga lishi yo,
Kogama iye kpadhishi otogu enwu li ununu yo,
Eblikpabi zhikeji yo dhuma awejita udor.

MH 106   O, How I Love Jesus   SDAH 248
Federick Whitfield, 1855 (1829-1904)
English

1
There is a name I love to hear,
I love to sing its worth;
It sounds like music in my ear,
The sweetest name on earth.

Chorus
O, how I love Jesus,
O, how I love Jesus,
O, how I love Jesus
Because He first Loved me!

2
It tells me of a Savior's love,
Who died to set me free;
It tells me of His precious blood,
The sinner's perfect plea.

3
It tells of One whose loving heart
Can feel my deepest woe,
Who in each sorrow bears apart
That none can bear below.

MH 106   O, How I Love Jesus   SDAH 248
Federick Whitfield, 1855 (1829-1904)
Ekpeye Translation

1
Uzhi ewa mor gwushi lu unuji,
Morgwushi lu uka kpu uzhile,
Ukpor kpormu uli uma le ete me,
Ewa kakpoligbe lu uwa.

2
Ugwushi me le Jesus,
Ugwushi me le Jesus,
Ugwushi me le Jesus,
Iye dor ya gwushi me luzu.

2
Ukani me ugwushi nyu ugawe,
Nye mu unwulor lu unama me le edhi,
Ukani me iye kpani ubala ma aya,
Edhor uma nyu umeyeshi.

3
Ukani me nye ekpema ugwushi ya,
Unwe ike ubuji eke iwene me,
Nye mu la agbezhi ubuji ibe,
Uzhe nye emedho lu uwa

MH 107 Jesus, With Thy Church Abide SDAH 374
Thomas B. Pollock (1836-1896)
English

1
Jesus, with Thy Church abide;
Be her Savior, Lord, and Guide,
While on earth her faith is tried:
We beseech Thee, hear us.

2
May her voice be ever clear,
Warning of a judgment near,
Telling of a Savior dear:
We beseech Thee, hear us.

3
May she guide the poor and blind,
Seek the lost until she find,
And the broken hearted bind:
We beseech Thee, hear us.

4
May she holy triumphs win,
Overthrow the hosts of sin,
Gather all the nations in,
We beseech Thee, hear us.

MH 107 Jesus, With Thy Church Abide SDAH 374

Thomas B. Pollock (1836-1896)

Ekpeye Translation

1
Jesus, nashi keji uzugbani yo,
Bu nyu ugawe, nye nwe li unyeka,
Lu uwa uwhetu ya nwe umama,
Ye ya dhor yo nujini ye.

2
Me mu ukpor sama uli Ya,
Ugbama ikpe zhi uzedhu,
Lu ukarlorshie iye kpani nyu ugawe,
Ye ya dhor yo nujini ye.

3
Me mu unyeke nye ogboyi li nye enyekpor,
Wudhiga nyo owulu tutu uweji ma,
Ukayite nye eke agbezhi uma,
Ye ya dhor yo nujini ye.

4
Me mu utu ugo le egwele,
Megbokpo ogbo emene umeyeshi,
Kporgbedhe kpo gbele gbele igbu uwadhi,
Ye ya dhor yo nujini ye.

MH 108   Shall We Gather at the River   SDAH 432

Robert Lowry, 1864 (1826-1899)

English

1
Shall we gather at the river,
where bright angel feet have trod,
with its crystal tide forever
flowing by the throne of God?

Chorus
Yes, we'll gather at the river,
the beautiful, the beautiful river;
gather with the saints at the river
that flows by the throne of God.

2
On the margin of the river,
washing up its silver spray,
we will walk and worship ever,
all the happy golden day.

3
Ere we reach the shining river,
lay we every burden down;
grace our spirits will deliver,
and provide a robe and crown.

4
Soon we'll reach the shining river,
soon our pilgrimage will cease;
soon our happy hearts will quiver
with the melody of peace.

MH 108   Shall We Gather at the River   SDAH 432

Robert Lowry, 1864 (1826-1899)

Ekpeye Translation

1
Agbagboni le olimini,
Adhi mu emene uzhi uma nuzo gbe,
Ya li mini usa orwayi mu ogbo ogbo,
Ugbalorshi la agida eze Eblikpabi?

Chorus
Ye ya agbagboni le olimini,
Olimini zorzor, Olimini mu zorzor,
Ye le emene uzhi uma agbagboni le olimini,
Gbalorshor la agida eze Eblikpabi.

2
Le ukwu olimini ya,
Usama epele unye ya,
Ye aso lu ukpenyidhidha,
Gbele gbele eye lu obu etor.

3
Maba dhuma olimini nyumalor,
Abu pete gbele gbele umekpeli ye,
Le ortizhi, uwa ye enye ugawe,
Ene kapa li okpulushi eze.

4
Eke akanutor adhuma olmini nyumalor ya,
Ntukor kpu uzhi uma ogbole,
Ntukor kpu ekpema etor ezigidhile,
Le orbu etor upadhi.

MH 109   The Old Rugged Cross   SDAH 159

George Bernard, 1913 1873-1958)

English

1
On a hill far away stood an old rugged cross,
The emblem of suffering and shame,
And I love that old cross where the dearest and best
For a world of lost sinners was slain.

Chorus
So I'll cherish the old rugged cross,
Till my trophies at last I lay down;
I will cling to the old rugged cross,
And exchange it some day for a crown.

2
Oh, that old rugged cross, so despised by the world,
Has a wondrous attraction for me,
For the dear Lamb of God left His glory above,
To bear it to dark Calvary.

3
To the old rugged cross I will ever be true,
Its shame and reproach gladly bear;
Then He'll call me some day to my home far away,
Where His glory forever I'll share.

MH 109   The Old Rugged Cross   SDAH 159

George Bernard, 1913 1873-1958)
 Ekpeye Translation

1
Le olu egbu zhi la akputor,
Adhim ushi uye li uka zhor,
Iye ugbushi eji akwukwu li iwene,
Morgwushi ushi uye li uka ya,
Adhim mu ugbor gbe,
Nwuje emene umeyeshi uwa.

Chorus
Ma padhiwe ukani ushi uye li uka ya,
Tutu magala iye ugbushi eji umegbo me,
Ma dabeni lu ukani ushi uye li uka ya,
Ma agbanyoa le eye lo okpulushi eze

2
Ukani ushi uye li uka, amu eluwa lorgbe,
Unwe eke iye untu le me,
Ugaga mu Eblikpabi usabete ete Ya lo olu,
Muba ta akwukwu lu ushi uye li uka.

3
Ukani ushi uye li uka, Me zhi le ishishuka,
Ukor li iwene me dhu ubuji,
Ohume le eye, lu udhor me zhi la akputor,
Adhi me ketuke lu upadhi ya.

MH 110 Come, Ye Thankful People SDAH 557

Henry Alford, 1844 (1810-1871)

English

1
Come, ye thankful people, come,
Raise the song of harvest home;
All is safely gathered in,
Ere the winter storms begin.
God our Maker doth provide
For our wants to be supplied;
Come to God's own temple, come;
Raise the song of harvest home!

2
We ourselves are God's own field,
Fruit unto His praise to yield;
Wheat and tares together sown,
Unto joy or sorrow grown;
First the blade and then the ear,
Then the full corn shall appear;
Grant, O harvest Lord, that we
Wholesome grain and pure may be.

3
For the Lord our God shall come,
And shall take His harvest home;
From His field shall purge away
All that doth offend, that day;
Give His angels charge at last
In the fire the tares to cast;
But the fruitful ears to store
In His garner evermore.

MH 110 Come, Ye Thankful People SDAH 557
Henry Alford, 1844 (1810-1871)
Ekpeye Translation

1
Jani, emene ukela, jani,
Gwu yani orbu ugu gbidhi udhor,
Gbele gbele agbe gbedhe kpolema,
Mu ukayi okidhika mubaja,
Eblikpabi, nyor kpuye orlorwe,
lu une ye iye ye awudhiga,
Ja lu Eblikpabi, ja,
Gwu yani orbu ugu gbidhi udhor.

2
Ye wewe abu ika Eblikpabi,
Ukpulushi mu ulorwor nedha upadhi,
Gbidhi la ata mu unu gbedhor gbe,
Zordhu gbe le obu etor li agbezhi,
Awu unuzu bu uhor mu ba dhuma ina ya,
Mu orka wewe muba lor,
Hwe, Nye nwe ye, ika mu anwor
Iye ika zuke mu zorgbe orzor.

3
Nye nwe ye, Eblikpabi eja,
Alawortor iye ika ye udhor,
Lime ika ya anamakpo,
Gbele gbele iye la mu amashela,
Enedhe emene uzhi uma ugbakpo,
Lime echi ushishigbe ata,
Amu ubor ugbeke gbe,
Li ika gbidhi orgwu orgwulu.

MH 110 Come, Ye Thankful People SDAH 557
Henry Alford, 1844 (1810-1871)
English

4
Then, thou church triumphant, come,
Raise the song of harvest home;
All are safely gathered in,
Free from sorrow, free from sin,
There, forever purified,
In God's garner to abide;
Come, ten thousand angels, come,
Raise the glorious harvest home!

MH 110 Come, Ye Thankful People SDAH 557
Henry Alford, 1844 (1810-1871)
Ekpeye Translation

4
Emene uzugbani tuyani ugo,
Gwu yani orbu ugu gbidhu udhor,
Gbele gbelem agbe ghedhe kpolema,
Uzhe li agbezhi, uzhe li umeyeshi,
Emekwa kpolegbe adhi ya,
Ezhorgbe le ekwe Eblikpabi,
Jani, unu kulu unu emene uzhi uma,
Gwu yani upadhi ugu gbidhi udhor.

MH 111   There Is a Fountain   SDAH 336

William Cooper, 1770 (1731-1800)

English

1

There is a fountain filled with blood drawn from Emmanuel's
veins;
and sinners plunged beneath that flood
lose all their guilty stains.
Lose all their guilty stains,
lose all their guilty stains;
and sinners plunged beneath that flood
lose all their guilty stains.

2

The dying thief rejoiced to see
that fountain in his day;
and there may I, though vile as he,
wash all my sins away.
Wash all my sins away,
wash all my sins away;
and there may I, though vile as he,
wash all my sins away.

3

Thou dying Lamb!, thy precious blood
shall never lose its power
till all the ransomed church of God
be saved, to sin no more.
Be saved, to sin no more,
be saved, to sin no more;
till all the ransomed church of God
be saved, to sin no more.

MH 111   There Is a Fountain   SDAH 336

William Cooper, 1770 (1731-1800)
Ekpeye Translation

1
Uzhi onwo mini yulu lu ubala,
Udortugbe le eli Immanuel,
Emene umeyeshi wudadhu gbe lime ya,
Samakpo gbe gbiyo gbe,
Samakpo gbe gbiyo gbe,
Samakpo gbe gbiyo gbe,
Emene umeyeshi wudadhu gbe lime ya,
Samakpo gbe gbiyo gbe.

2
Nyu ugbu mu nwulor tor ekpema tuweji,
Onwo mini ya le eye ya,
Adhi me mu zhor, uyor gbiyor kpormu ya,
Usamakpo umeyeshi me,
Usamakpo umeyeshi me,
Usamakpo umeyeshi me,
Adhi mu me zhor, uyorgbiyor kpormu ya,
Usamakpo umeyeshi me.

3
Ugaga mu unwolor, ubala mu ugba aya,
Ndeke ugbakpo ya adada,
Gbele gbele uzugbani Eblikpabi unwor,
Ordolegbe umeyeshie dhegbe,
Ordolegbe umeyeshie dhegbe,
Ordolegbe umeyeshie dhegbe,
Gbele gbele uzugbani Eblikpabi unwor,
Ordolegbe umeyeshie dhegbe.

MH 111   There Is a Fountain   SDAH 336
William Cooper, 1770 (1731-1800)
English

4
E'er since, by faith, I saw the stream
thy flowing wounds supply,
Redeeming love has been my theme,
and shall be till I die.
And shall be till I die,
and shall be till I die;
redeeming love has been my theme,
and shall be till I die.

5
Lord, I believe Thou hast prepared,
unworthy though I be,
For me a blood-bought free reward,
a golden harp for me!
A golden harp for me!
A golden harp for me!
For me a blood-bought free reward,
a golden harp for me!

6
There in a nobler, sweeter song,
I'll sing Thy power to save,
When this poor lisping, stammering tongue
Is ransomed from the grave.
Is ransomed from the grave,
Is ransomed from the grace;
When this poor lisping, stammering tongue
Is ransomed from the grave.

MH 111   There Is a Fountain   SDAH 336

William Cooper, 1770 (1731-1800)

Ekpeye Translation

4
Tutum, lu uwhetu me weji mini ya,
Adhim mu enye yo lor,
Ugwushi udorkpewe bu iye ekpor me,
Me zhi tutu nnwulu,
Me zhi tutu nnwulu,
Me zhi tutu nnwulu,
Ugwushi udorkpewe bu iye ckpor me,
Me zhi tutu nnwulu.

5
Nye nwe ye, me whe, gbuyo ejikele kpole,
Me wheshe mu lu uzhi,
Ugo gbe me lu ubala ewe,
Ubor gold bu ame,
Ubor gold bu ame,
Ubor gold bu ame,
Ugo gbe me lu ubala ewe,
Ubor gold bu ame.

6
Uzhi orbu bu eke utor etor,
Mor orgwu lu kala ugbakpo yo,
Kpormu nyu uya, nye idho ibenwa
Ugo agbe le eka ili,
Ugo agbe le eka ili,
Ugo agbe le eka ili,
Kpormu nyu uya, nye idho ibenwa,
Ugo agbe le eka ili.

MH 112   Because He Lives   SDAH 526
Gloria Gaither, 1971 (1942-)
William J. Gaither, 1971
English

1
God sent His Son, they called Him Jesus,
He came to love, heal, and forgive;
He lived and died to buy my pardon,
An empty grave is there to prove my Savior
lives.

Chorus
Because He lives I can face tomorrow,
Because He lives all fear is gone;
Because I know He holds the future.
And life is worth the living just because He lives

2
How sweet to hold a newborn baby,
And feel the pride, and joy He gives;
But greater still the calm assurance,
This child can face uncertain days because He
lives.

MH 112   Because He Lives   SDAH 526

Gloria Gaither, 1971 (1942-)
William J. Gaither, 1971
Ekpeye Translation

1
Eblikpabi zewe unwor Ya,
Uwhu agbe Jesus
Ujanyi ugwushi, ugwor li ortizhi
Ube mu unwulor lu ugo usabeteni me
Okpokolo ili, zhi lu ukalorshie,
Nye nwe mc zhim

Chorus
Iyedor uzhim, mo nuzo nyidho sele,
Iyedor uzhim, otogu agale,
Iyedor ma amajor, umojike iye ununu,
Budu zhihor, la ube lu umorm, Iyedor uzhim.

2
Ndekpu etor uwhuji, unwor uwu zhile,
Lu uzhi li ime ide, obu etor nedhi,
Awu kakpoligbe, egba uyodu,
Unworm nuzo nyidho eye amaje,
Iyedor uzhim.

MH 113   Worthy, Worthy Is the Lamb   SDAH 246

Anonymous

English

1
Worthy, worthy is the Lamb,
Worthy, worthy is the Lamb,
Worthy, worthy is the Lamb,
That was slain.

Chorus
Glory, hallelujah!
Praise Him, hallelujah!
Glory, hallelujah!
To the Lamb!

2
Savior, let Thy kingdom come!
Now the power of sin consume;
Bring Thy blest millennium,
Holy Lamb.

3
Thus may we each moment feel,
Love Him, serve Him,
praise Him still,
Till we all on Zion's hill
See the Lamb.

MH 113 Worthy, Worthy Is the Lamb SDAH 246
Anonymous
Ekpeye Translation

1
Uwheshi, uwheshi bu ugagam,
Uwheshi, uwheshi bu ugagam,
Uwheshi, uwheshi bu ugagam,
Ugbor gbe.

Chorus
Padhi, Al-le-lu-jah,
Padhiwe anyi, Al-le lu-jah,
Padhi, Al-le-lu-jah,
Padhiweni ugaga.

2
Nye ugawe ele eze yo ja,
Ugbakpo umeyeshi orgwulule,
Gala, unu kulu unu ala,
Ugaga zhi egwele.

3
Ye le gbele gbele ekele azhi,
Lu ugwusha, akpenya, apadhiwa,
Dhuma ekele gbele gbele ye, le egbu Zion,
Aweji ugaga ya.

MH 114   Hold Fast Till I Come ...SDAH 600

F. E. Belden, 1886 (1858-1945)

English

1
Sweet promise is given to all who believe--
"Behold I come quickly, Mine own to receive;
Hold fast till I come; the danger is great;
Sleep not as do others; be watchful, and wait."

Chorus
"Hold fast till I come," sweet promise of heaven--
"The kingdom restored, to you shall be given."
"Come, enter My joy, sit down on the throne;
Bright crowns are in waiting; hold fast till I come."

2
We'll "watch unto prayer" with lamps burning bright;
He comes to all others a "thief in the night."
We know He is near, but know not the day--
As spring shows that summer is not far away.

3
Yes! this is our hope, 'tis built on His word--
The glorious appearing of Jesus, our Lord;
Of promises all, it stands as the sum:
"Behold I come quickly; hold fast till I come."

MH 114   Hold Fast Till I Come ...SDAH 600
F. E. Belden, 1886 (1858-1945)
Ekpeye Translation

1
Egbe etor mu unegbe emene mu uwhetugbe—
Notu, mezhi lu uja enwa, lu ugonu ame,
Mojike tutu nja, Iye otogu ubu eke,
Esator ude emene nyigbe nyina.

Chorus
Mojike tutu nja, egba etor mu orbioma--
Ele ezem uno-osagbe, enegbe bu yo,
Kpudhu le obu etor me, Nuzhi la agida eze me,
Okpulushi eze dhuseji; mojike tutu nja

2
Seji lime edhor, leke tunjo dhu unwu,
Ujakeji gbele gbele emene, kpormu nyu ugbu la abali,
Amaji gbuzhi uzedhu, agwe hutor umaji eye ya—
Kpormu ulamini tugoshor utala, uzhe la akputor.

3
Omu ubu unye enye ye, unu agbe lu unu ekpor ya—
Igili ujeja, amu nye Nwe ye, Jesus,
Amu gbele gbele egba, Unuzo gbedhe uwadhi,
Nye nwe me zhi luja enwa, Mojike tutu nja.

MH 115   I Will Follow Thee SDAH 623

James Lawson Elginburg, 1886

English

1
I will follow Thee, my Savior,
Wheresoe'er my lot may be.
Where thou goest I will follow;
Yes, my Lord, I'll follow Thee.

Chorus
I will follow Thee, my Saviour,
Thou didst shed Thy blood for me;
And though all men should forsake Thee;
By Thy grace I'll follow Thee.
2
Though the road be rough and thorny,
Trackless as the foaming sea,
Thou hast trod this way before me,
And I'll gladly follow Thee.
3
Though I meet with tribulations,
Sorely tempted though I be;
I remember Thou wast tempted,
And rejoice to follow Thee.
4
Though Thou leadest me through affliction,
Poor, forsaken though I be;
Thou wast destitute, afflicted,
And I only follow Thee.

5
Though to Jordan's rolling billows,
Cold and deep, Thou leadest me,
Thou hast crossed the waves before me,
And I still will follow Thee.

MH 115   I Will Follow Thee SDAH 623
James Lawson Elginburg, 1886
Ekpeye Translation

1
Me echiya yo, nyu ugawe me,
Ladhi uwhe kala nyi le me,
Adhi izele, me echiya Yo,
Nye nwe me, me echiya Yo.

Chorus
Me echiya Yo, nyu ugawe me,
Kpormu iwosa uhala yo le me,
Umashi gbu gbele gbele madu lorgbe Yo,
Lor ortizhi yo me echiya Yo.
2
Ichakpa ya, uyor gbiyo, uzhi ugwu,
Uzhidhiga kpormu uwuluwulu mini,
Ye kaze male ichakpa lu unuzu,
Me echiya le obu etor.

3
Umeshi me weji eke umekpeli,
Legedhe, me zhi lu umama,
Me gbeweji amakpo legbe Yo,
Le obu etor, me echiya Yo
4
Yo idulaga me le akwukwu,
Morbu nyu uya li nyu ulorgbe orlor,
Yo ezhimale le eke ukor li akwukwu,
Me neten me echiya yo.
5
Eke orwaji olimini Jordan,
Ukayi li udhu, idulaga me,
Ye ewekpowele orwayi ya le unuzu,
Me echiya keji hutor bu Yo.

MH 116   Great Is Thy Faithfulness … SDAH 100
Thomas O. Chisholm, 1923 (1866-1960)
William O. Runyan, 1925 (1870-1957)
English

1
Great is Thy faithfulness, O God my Father;
There is no shadow of turning with Thee;
Thou changest not, Thy compassions, they fail not;
As Thou hast been, Thou forever will be.

Chorus
Great is Thy faithfulness!
Great is Thy faithfulness!
Morning by morning new mercies I see.
All I have needed Thy hand hath provided;
Great is Thy faithfulness, Lord, unto me!

2
Summer and winter and springtime and harvest,
Sun, moon and stars in their courses above
Join with all nature in manifold witness
To Thy great faithfulness, mercy and love.

3
Pardon for sin and a peace that endureth
Thine own dear presence to cheer and to guide;
Strength for today and bright hope for tomorrow,
Blessings all mine, with ten thousand beside!

MH 116   Great Is Thy Faithfulness ... SDAH 100
Thomas O. Chisholm, 1923 (1866-1960)
William O. Runyan, 1925 (1870-1957)
Ekpeye Translation

1
Uwhetu ubu eke, Eblikpabi Eda me;
Inwe ugbanyo li ime Yo
Yo igbanyor ortizhi Yo ogbo ogbo,
Kpormu izhor, akpu izhi dhidhile

Chorus
Eke uwhetu Yo!
Eke uwhetu Yo!
Gbele gbele oyukwe ortizhi uwu me weji,
Iye mo wudhiga eke yo enekpoleme;
Eke uwhetu Yo, Nye nwe me neh me.

2
Utala, uwoni, ulamini li ugugbidhi,
Elanwu, ada-igwe, okpudhor egbu-luka lu ugbolo-gbe
Uzhigbe le iye lorwe eka ugbolo Eblikpabi,
Le eke uwhetu Yo, ortizhi li ugwushi

3
Usabeteni umeyeshi li uyodhu ukayite uma,
Le ununu Yo inyeke li ugbayiteke;
Ugbakpo li tam li unye enye uma sele,
Uwokpani mu ame li unu kulu unu uzhagbe!

MH 117 There Is a Green Hill Far Away SDAH 164
Cecil Francis Alexander, 1848 (1818-1895)
English

1
There is a green hill far away,
Without a city wall,
Where the dear Lord was crucified,
Who died to save us all.

2
We may not know, we cannot tell,
What pains He had to bear,
But we believe it was for us,
He hung and suffered there.

3
He died that we might be forgiven,
He died to make us good,
That we might go at last to heaven,
Saved by His precious blood.

4
There was no other good enough
To pay the price of sin;
He only could unlock the gate
Of heaven, and let us in.

5
O dearly, dearly has He loved!
And we must love Him too,
And trust in His redeeming blood,
And try His works to do.

MH 117 There Is a Green Hill Far Away SDAH 164
Cecil Francis Alexander, 1848 (1818-1895)
Ekpeye Translation

1
Egbu zhi lo okpe akputor,
Lu ulamu egbeleta ezhe,
Adhimu ukporgbogbe Nye nwe ye,
Nye mu unwulor lu udor ye.

2
Ye amaje, ndeke ye akadhor,
Kpu edhe ya dhelema,
Ye awhetu gbubu lishi ye,
Mu ukonyor li ushi mu uta akwukwu.

3
Unwulu lishi usabeteni ye,
Unwulu meke amunu,
Mu umanu akaze ele eze,
Udor ye lu ubala uma ya.

4
Uzhe iye gbumagba ga,
Lu uwhudhiwe ugwor umeyeshi,
Ya neten echima egbeleta,
Ele eze meke akpudhi.

5
Eke ugwushi, eke ugwushim ugwushor,
Ye ya agwushi dhiwani kpe,
Ashishi unukwuma le ubala ugawe mu Aya,
Ma agbake lu ume ugbolo Ya.

MH 118 Now Thank We All Our God   SDAH 559

Martin Rinkleri, 1636 (1586-1649)
Tr. by Catherine Winkworth, 1858 (1827-1878)
English

1
Now thank we all our God
with heart and hands and voices,
who wondrous things hath done,
in whom His world rejoices;
Who, from our mothers' arms
hath blessed us on our way
with countless gifts of love,
and still is ours today.

2
O may this bounteous God
through all our life be near us,
with ever joyful hearts
and blessed peace to cheer us;
and keep us still in grace,
and guide us when perplexed;
and free us from all ills,
in this world and the next.

3
All praise and thanks to God
the Father now be given;
the Son, and Him who reigns
with them in highest heaven;
the one eternal God,
whom earth and heaven adore;
for thus it was, is now,
and shall be evermore.

MH 118 Now Thank We All Our God   SDAH 559

Martin Rinkleri, 1636 (1586-1649)
Tr.by Catherine Winkworth, 1858 (1827-1878)

Ekpeye Translation

1
Ye akela Eblikpabi lu umorm,
Le ekpema li eka li obu,
Nye meh iye unyodhawe enye,
Le nyem eluwa padhorgbe,
Nye mu le eka ena ye,
Uwokwani ichakpa ye,
Lu ugwushi enwe ugwu orgwu,
Dhuzhi nyi dhihu ye.

2
Eblikpabi uma mu,
Zhini ye le ekidhi budu ye,
Le ekpema etor mu ogbo ogbo,
Lu uwokwani uyodhu ukayite obu,
Mugbeye lu ortizhi Ya,
Mu nyeke ye lawu ukelike,
Mu unama ye la akwukwu,
Lu uwam li ame ejom.

3
Upadhi li ukela bu awu Eblikpabi,
Unegbe Eda lu umormu,
Unwor li Nye chikejigbe,
Le orbioma mu ukakpoliogbe,
Eblikpabim Ya neten zhor;
Eluwa li orbioma kpenyor gbe;
Amu uzhor, mu uzhe lu morm,
Dhuma ekele ogbo ogbo.

MH 119   Lead Them, My God, to Thee SDAH 653
F. E. Belden, 1886 (1858-1945)
English

1
Lead them, my God, to Thee, Lead them to Thee,
These children dear of mine, Thou gavest me;
O, by Thy love divine, Lead them, my God, to Thee;
Lead them, my God, to Thee, Lead them to Thee.

2
When earth looks bright and fair, Festive and gay,
Let no delusive snare Lure them astray;
But from temptation's power, Lead them, my God, to Thee,
Lead them, my God, to Thee, Lead them to Thee.

3
E'en for such little ones, Christ came a child,
And in this world of sin Lived undefiled.
O, for His sake, I pray, Lead them, my God, to Thee,
Lead them, my God, to Thee, Lead them to Thee.

4
Yea, though my faith be dim, I would believe,
That Thou this precious gift Wilt now receive;
O take their young hearts now, Lead them my God to Thee,
Lead them, my God, to Thee, Lead them to Thee.

MH 119   Lead Them, My God, to Thee SDAH 653
F. E. Belden, 1886 (1858-1945)
Ekpeye Translation

1
Dutugbe Eblikpabi, dutugbe,
Umeledhe mu uzhigbe me lu uwa, Yo inegbe me,
Lu ugwushi uwuma Yo,
Dutugbe Eblikpabi, Dutugbe Eblikpabi, dutugbe.

2
Let uwa gamalile, upadhi li obu etor,
Ewhe gbu unagbo uwa dorlawcgbc orzu
Dorkpewegbe le ugbakpo umama,
Dutugbe Eblikpabi, dutugbe Eblikpabi, dutugbe.

3
Umashi ubu otu ntukorm, Christ jazu umeledhe,
Li ime uwa umeyeshim, Udhuma eliya,
Le ishi Ya abu iye mordhor nyi,
Dutugbe Eblikpabi, dutugbe Eblikpabi, dutugbe.

4
Umashi uwhetu me zhili igeleni, me ewhe bu ewhe,
Gbuyo, enator lu umorm, egwuma uma,
Gonu ekpema uwu gbe lu umorm,
Dutugbe Eblikpabi, dutugbe Eblikpabi, dutugbe.

MH 120   The Lord is in His Temple   SDAH 692
George F. Roots (1820-1895)
English

The Lord is in His holy temple,
The Lord is in His temple,
Let all the earth keep silence,
Let all the earth keep silence before him,
Keep silence before him.
Amen.

MH 120   The Lord is in His Temple   SDAH 692
George F. Roots (1820-1895)
Ekpeye Translation

Nye nwe ye zhi lu udhor egwele Ya,
Nye nwe ye zhi lu udhor egwele Ya,
Eluwa ekporni ekpor,
Eluwa ekporni ekpor lu ununu Ya,
Ekporni lu ununu Ya.
Uzhe-kpeye

MH 121   Glory Be to the Father   SDAH 660
H. W. Greatorex, 1851 (1811-1858)
English

Glory be to the Father and to the son,
And to the Holy Ghost;
As it was in the beginning, is now and
ever shall be, world without end.
Amen, amen.

MH 121   Glory Be to the Father   SDAH 660
H. W. Greatorex, 1851 (1811-1858)
Ekpeye Translation

Upadhiwe zhini Eda
Li unwor, li uwazhi Egwele,
Kpormu uzhe nu unuzu, mu uzhor lu umorm,
dhuma eluwa orgwulu orgwulu,
u-u-zhi kpe-ye.

High Chief Nyamanunyi Miller Tobia Solomon
July 2, 1929, to July 5, 2021
Author & Translator

Made in the USA
Columbia, SC
19 March 2024

33104687R00153